William Shakespeare

LOVE'S LABOR'S LOST

With New Dramatic Criticism
and an Updated Bibliography

Edited by John Arthos

The Signet Classic Shakespeare
GENERAL EDITOR: SYLVAN BARNET

A SIGNET CLASSIC

SIGNET CLASSIC
Published by the Penguin Group
Penguin Books USA Inc., 375 Hudson Street,
New York, New York 10014, U.S.A.
Penguin Books Ltd, 27 Wrights Lane,
London W8 5TZ, England
Penguin Books Australia Ltd, Ringwood,
Victoria, Australia
Penguin Books Canada Ltd, 10 Alcorn Avenue,
Toronto, Ontario, Canada M4V 3B2
Penguin Books (N.Z.) Ltd, 182–190 Wairau Road,
Auckland 10, New Zealand

Penguin Books Ltd, Registered Offices:
Harmondsworth, Middlesex, England

Published by Signet Classic, an imprint of Dutton Signet,
a division of Penguin Books USA Inc.

19   18   17   16   15

Library of Congress Catalog Card Number: 88-61105

Printed in the United States of America

Contents

Shakespeare: Prefatory Remarks

Between the record of his baptism in Stratford on 26 April 1564 and the record of his burial in Stratford on 25 April 1616, some forty documents name Shakespeare, and many others name his parents, his children, and his grandchildren. More facts are known about William Shakespeare than about any other playwright of the period except Ben Jonson. The facts should, however, be distinguished from the legends. The latter, inevitably more engaging and better known, tell us that the Stratford boy killed a calf in high style, poached deer and rabbits, and was forced to flee to London, where he held horses outside a playhouse. These traditions are only traditions; they may be true, but no evidence supports them, and it is well to stick to the facts.

Mary Arden, the dramatist's mother, was the daughter of a substantial landowner; about 1557 she married John Shakespeare, who was a glove-maker and trader in various farm commodities. In 1557 John Shakespeare was a member of the Council (the governing body of Stratford), in 1558 a constable of the borough, in 1561 one of the two town chamberlains, in 1565 an alderman (entitling him to the appellation "Mr."), in 1568 high bailiff—the town's highest political office, equivalent to mayor. After 1577, for an unknown reason he drops out of local politics. The birthday of William Shakespeare, the eldest son of this locally prominent man, is unrecorded; but the Stratford parish register records that the infant was baptized on 26

April 1564. (It is quite possible that he was born on 23 April, but this date has probably been assigned by tradition because it is the date on which, fifty-two years later, he died.) The attendance records of the Stratford grammar school of the period are not extant, but it is reasonable to assume that the son of a local official attended the school and received substantial training in Latin. The masters of the school from Shakespeare's seventh to fifteenth years held Oxford degrees; the Elizabethan curriculum excluded mathematics and the natural sciences but taught a good deal of Latin rhetoric, logic, and literature. On 27 November 1582 a marriage license was issued to Shakespeare and Anne Hathaway, eight years his senior. The couple had a child in May, 1583. Perhaps the marriage was necessary, but perhaps the couple had earlier engaged in a formal "troth plight" which would render their children legitimate even if no further ceremony were performed. In 1585 Anne Hathaway bore Shakespeare twins.

That Shakespeare was born is excellent; that he married and had children is pleasant; but that we know nothing about his departure from Stratford to London, or about the beginning of his theatrical career, is lamentable and must be admitted. We would gladly sacrifice details about his children's baptism for details about his earliest days on the stage. Perhaps the poaching episode is true (but it is first reported almost a century after Shakespeare's death), or perhaps he first left Stratford to be a schoolteacher, as another tradition holds; perhaps he was moved by

> Such wind as scatters young men through the world,
> To seek their fortunes further than at home
> Where small experience grows.

In 1592, thanks to the cantankerousness of Robert Greene, a rival playwright and a pamphleteer, we have our first reference, a snarling one, to Shakespeare as an actor and playright. Greene warns those of his own educated friends who wrote for the theater against an actor who has presumed to turn playwright:

There is an upstart crow, beautified with our feathers, that with his *tiger's heart wrapped in a player's hide* supposes he is as well able to bombast out a blank verse as the best of you, and being an absolute Johannes-facto-tum is in his own conceit the only Shake-scene in a country.

The reference to the player, as well as the allusion to Aesop's crow (who strutted in borrowed plumage, as an actor struts in fine words not his own), makes it clear that by this date Shakespeare had both acted and written. That Shakespeare is meant is indicated not only by "Shake-scene" but by the parody of a line from one of Shakespeare's plays, *3 Henry VI:* "O, tiger's heart wrapped in a woman's hide." If Shakespeare in 1592 was prominent enough to be attacked by an envious dram-atist, he probably had served an apprenticeship in the theater for at least a few years.

In any case, by 1592 Shakespeare had acted and writ-ten, and there are a number of subsequent references to him as an actor: documents indicate that in 1598 he is a "principal comedian," in 1603 a "principal tragedian," in 1608 he is one of the "men players." The profession of actor was not for a gentleman, and it occasionally drew the scorn of university men who resented writing speeches for persons less educated than themselves, but it was re-spectable enough: players, if prosperous, were in effect members of the bourgeoisie, and there is nothing to sug-gest that Stratford considered William Shakespeare less than a solid citizen. When, in 1596, the Shakespeares were granted a coat of arms, the grant was made to Shake-speare's father, but probably William Shakespeare (who the next year bought the second-largest house in town) had arranged the matter on his own behalf. In subsequent transactions he is occasionally styled a gentleman.

Although in 1593 and 1594 Shakespeare published two narrative poems dedicated to the Earl of Southampton, *Venus and Adonis* and *The Rape of Lucrece,* and may well have written most or all of his sonnets in the middle nineties, Shakespeare's literary activity seems to have been almost entirely devoted to the theater. (It may be significant that the two narrative poems were written in years when the plague closed the theaters for several months.) In 1594 he was a charter member of a theatrical company called the Chamberlain's Men (which in 1603 changed its name to the King's Men); until he retired to Stratford (about 1611, apparently), he was with this remarkably stable company. From 1599 the company acted primarily at the Globe Theatre, in which Shakespeare held a one-tenth interest. Other Elizabethan dramatists are known to have acted, but no other is known also to have been entitled to a share in the profits of the playhouse.

Shakespeare's first eight published plays did not have his name on them, but this is not remarkable; the most popular play of the sixteenth century, Thomas Kyd's *The Spanish Tragedy,* went through many editions without naming Kyd, and Kyd's authorship is known only because a book on the profession of acting happens to quote (and attribute to Kyd) some lines on the interest of Roman emperors in the drama. What is remarkable is that after 1598 Shakespeare's name commonly appears on printed plays—some of which are not his. Another indication of his popularity comes from Francis Meres, author of *Palladis Tamia: Wit's Treasury* (1598): in this anthology of snippets accompanied by an essay on literature, many playwrights are mentioned, but Shakespeare's name occurs more often than any other, and Shakespeare is the only playwright whose plays are listed.

From his acting, playwriting, and share in a theater, Shakespeare seems to have made considerable money. He put it to work, making substantial investments in Stratford real estate. When he made his will (less than a month before he died), he sought to leave his property intact to his descendants. Of small bequests to relatives and to friends (including three actors, Richard Burbage, John Heminges, and Henry Condell), that to his wife of the second-best bed has provoked the most comment; perhaps it was the bed the couple had slept in, the best being reserved for visitors. In any case, had Shakespeare not excepted it, the bed would have gone (with the rest of his

household possessions) to his daughter and her husband.
On 25 April 1616 he was buried within the chancel of
the church at Stratford. An unattractive monument to his
memory, placed on a wall near the grave, says he died
on 23 April. Over the grave itself are the lines, perhaps
by Shakespeare, that (more than his literary fame) have
kept his bones undisturbed in the crowded burial ground
where old bones were often dislodged to make way for
new:

> Good friend, for Jesus' sake forbear
> To dig the dust enclosèd here.
> Blessed be the man that spares these stones
> And cursed be he that moves my bones.

Thirty-seven plays, as well as some nondramatic poems,
are held to constitute the Shakespeare canon. The dates of
composition of most of the works are highly uncertain,
but there is often evidence of a *terminus a quo* (starting
point) and/or a *terminus ad quem* (terminal point) that
provides a framework for intelligent guessing. For example, *Richard II* cannot be earlier than 1595, the publication date of some material to which it is indebted; *The
Merchant of Venice* cannot be later than 1598, the year
Francis Meres mentioned it. Sometimes arguments for a
date hang on an alleged topical allusion, such as the lines
about the unseasonable weather in *A Midsummer Night's
Dream,* II.i.81–117, but such an allusion (if indeed it is an
allusion) can be variously interpreted, and in any case
there is always the possibility that a topical allusion was
inserted during a revision, years after the composition of
a play. Dates are often attributed on the basis of style,
and although conjectures about style usually rest on other
conjectures, sooner or later one must rely on one's literary
sense. There is no real proof, for example, that *Othello* is
not as early as *Romeo and Juliet,* but one feels *Othello*
is later, and because the first record of its performance
is 1604, one is glad enough to set its composition at that
date and not push it back into Shakespeare's early years.
The following chronology, then, is as much indebted to

informed guesswork and sensitivity as it is to fact. The dates, necessarily imprecise, indicate something like a scholarly consensus.

PLAYS

1588–93	*The Comedy of Errors*
1588–94	*Love's Labor's Lost*
1590–91	*2 Henry VI*
1590–91	*3 Henry VI*
1591–92	*1 Henry VI*
1592–93	*Richard III*
1592–94	*Titus Andronicus*
1593–94	*The Taming of the Shrew*
1593–95	*The Two Gentlemen of Verona*
1594–96	*Romeo and Juliet*
1595	*Richard II*
1594–96	*A Midsummer Night's Dream*
1596–97	*King John*
1596–97	*The Merchant of Venice*
1597	*1 Henry IV*
1597–98	*2 Henry IV*
1598–99	*Henry V*
1598–1600	*Much Ado About Nothing*
1599	*Julius Caesar*
1599–1600	*As You Like it*
1599–1600	*Twelfth Night*
1600–01	*Hamlet*
1597–1601	*The Merry Wives of Windsor*
1601–02	*Troilus and Cressida*
1602–04	*All's Well That Ends Well*
1603–04	*Othello*
1604	*Measure for Measure*
1605–06	*King Lear*
1605–06	*Macbeth*
1606–07	*Antony and Cleopatra*
1605–08	*Timon of Athens*
1607–09	*Coriolanus*
1608–09	*Pericles*

1609–10	*Cymbeline*
1610–11	*The Winter's Tale*
1611	*The Tempest*
1612–13	*Henry VIII*

POEMS

1592	*Venus and Adonis*
1593–94	*The Rape of Lucrece*
1593–1600	*Sonnets*
1600–01	*The Phoenix and the Turtle*

Shakespeare's Theater

In Shakespeare's infancy, Elizabethan actors performed wherever they could—in great halls, at court, in the court-yards of inns. The innyards must have made rather un-satisfactory theaters: on some days they were unavailable because carters bringing goods to London used them as depots; when available, they had to be rented from the innkeeper; perhaps most important, London inns were subject to the Common Council of London, which was not well disposed toward theatricals. In 1574 the Common Council required that plays and playing places in London be licensed. It asserted that

> sundry great disorders and inconveniences have been found to ensue to this city by the inordinate haunting of great multitudes of people, specially youth, to plays, interludes, and shows, namely occasion of frays and quarrels, evil practices of incontinency in great inns having chambers and secret places adjoining to their open stages and galleries,

and ordered that innkeepers who wished licenses to hold performances put up a bond and make contributions to the poor.

The requirement that plays and innyard theaters be licensed, along with the other drawbacks of playing at inns, probably drove James Burbage (a carpenter-turned-actor) to rent in 1576 a plot of land northeast of the city walls and to build here—on property outside the jurisdiction of the city—England's first permanent construction designed for plays. He called it simply the Theatre. About all that is known of its construction is that it was wood. It soon had imitators, the most famous being the Globe (1599), built across the Thames (again outside the city's jurisdiction), out of timbers of the Theatre, which had been dismantled when Burbage's lease ran out.

There are three important sources of information about the structure of Elizabethan playhouses—drawings, a contract, and stage directions in plays. Of drawings, only the so-called De Witt drawing (c. 1596) of the Swan—really a friend's copy of De Witt's drawing—is of much significance. It shows a building of three tiers, with a stage jutting from a wall into the yard or center of the building. The tiers are roofed, and part of the stage is covered by a roof that projects from the rear and is supported at its front on two posts, but the groundlings, who paid a penny to stand in front of the stage, were exposed to the sky. (Performances in such a playhouse were held only in the daytime; artificial illumination was not used.) At the rear of the stage are two doors; above the stage is a gallery. The second major source of information, the contract for the Fortune, specifies that although the Globe is to be the model, the Fortune is to be square, eighty feet outside and fifty-five inside. The stage is to be forty-three feet broad, and is to extend into the middle of the yard (i.e., it is twenty-seven and a half feet deep). For patrons willing to pay more than the general admission charged of the groundlings, there were to be three galleries provided with seats. From the third chief source, stage directions, one learns that entrance to the stage was by doors, presumably spaced widely apart at the rear ("Enter one citizen at one door, and another at the other"), and that in addition to the platform stage there was occasionally some sort of curtained booth or alcove allowing for "discovery" scenes, and some sort of playing space "aloft" or "above" to represent (for example) the top of a city's walls or a room above the street. Doubtless each theater had its own peculiarities, but perhaps we can talk about a "typical" Elizabethan theater if we realize that no theater need exactly have fit the description, just as no father is the typical father with 3.7 children. This hypothetical theater is wooden, round or polygonal (in *Henry V* Shakespeare calls it a "wooden *O*"), capable of holding some eight hundred spectators standing in the yard around the projecting elevated stage and some fifteen hundred additional spectators seated in the three roofed galleries. The stage, protected by a "shadow" or "heavens" or roof, is entered by two doors; behind the doors is the "tiring house" (attiring house, i.e., dressing room), and above the doors is some sort of gallery that may sometimes hold spectators but that can be used (for example) as the bedroom from which Romeo—according to a stage direction in one text—"goeth down." Some evidence suggests that a throne can be lowered onto the platform stage, perhaps from the "shadow"; certainly characters can descend from the stage through a trap or traps into the cellar or "hell." Sometimes this space beneath the platform accommodates a sound-effects man or musician (in *Antony and Cleopatra* "music of the hautboys is under the stage") or an actor (in *Hamlet* the "Ghost cries under the stage"). Most characters simply walk on and off, but because there is no curtain in front of the platform, corpses will have to be carried off (Hamlet must lug Polonius' guts into the neighbor room), or will have to fall at the rear, where the curtain on the alcove or booth can be drawn to conceal them.

Such may have been the so-called "public theater." Another kind of theater, called the "private theater" because its much greater admission charge limited its audience to the wealthy or the prodigal, must be briefly mentioned. The private theater was basically a large room, entirely roofed and therefore artificially illuminated, with a stage at one end. In 1576 one such theater was established in Blackfriars, a Dominican priory in London that had been suppressed in 1538 and confiscated by the Crown and thus was not under the city's jurisdiction. All the actors in the Blackfriars theater were boys about eight to thirteen years old (in the public theaters similar boys played female parts; a boy Lady Macbeth played to a man Macbeth). This private theater had a precarious existence, and ceased operations in 1584. In 1596 James Burbage, who had already made theatrical history by building the Theatre, began to construct a second Blackfriars theater. He died in 1597, and for several years this second Blackfriars theater was used by a troupe of boys, but in 1608 two of Burbage's sons and five other actors (including Shakespeare) became joint operators of the theater, using it in the winter when the open-air Globe was unsuitable. Perhaps such a smaller theater, roofed, artificially illuminated, and with a tradition of a courtly audience, exerted an influence on Shakespeare's late plays.

Performances in the private theaters may well have had intermissions during which music was played, but in the public theaters the action was probably uninterrupted, flowing from scene to scene almost without a break. Actors would enter, speak, exit, and others would immediately enter and establish (if necessary) the new locale by a few properties and by words and gestures. Here are some samples of Shakespeare's scene painting:

This is Illyria, lady.

Well, this is the Forest of Arden.

This castle hath a pleasant seat; the air
Nimbly and sweetly recommends itself
Unto our gentle senses.

On the other hand, it is a mistake to conceive of the Elizabethan stage as bare. Although Shakespeare's Chorus in *Henry V* calls the stage an "unworthy scaffold" and urges the spectators to "eke out our performance with your mind," there was considerable spectacle. The last act of *Macbeth,* for example, has five stage directions calling for "drum and colors," and another sort of appeal to the eye is indicated by the stage direction "Enter Macduff, with Macbeth's head." Some scenery and properties may have been substantial; doubtless a throne was used, and in one play of the period we encounter this direction: "Hector takes up a great piece of rock and casts at Ajax, who tears up a young tree by the roots and assails Hector." The matter is of some importance, and will be glanced at again in the next section.

The Texts of Shakespeare

Though eighteen of his plays were published during his lifetime, Shakespeare seems never to have supervised their publication. There is nothing unusual here; when a playwright sold a play to a theatrical company he surrendered his ownership of it. Normally a company would not publish the play, because to publish it meant to allow competitors to acquire the piece. Some plays, however, did get published: apparently treacherous actors sometimes pieced together a play for a publisher, sometimes a company in need of money sold a play, and sometimes a company allowed a play to be published that no longer drew audiences. That Shakespeare did not concern himself with publication, then, is scarcely remarkable; of his contemporaries only Ben Jonson carefully supervised the publication of his own plays. In 1623, seven years after Shakespeare's death, John Heminges and Henry Condell (two senior members of Shakespeare's company, who had performed with him for about twenty years) collected his plays—published and unpublished—into a large volume, commonly called the First Folio. (A folio is a volume consisting of sheets that have been folded once, each sheet thus making two leaves, or four pages. The eighteen plays published during Shakespeare's lifetime had been issued one play per volume in small books called quartos. Each sheet in a quarto has been folded twice, making four leaves, or eight pages.) The First Folio contains thirty-six plays; a thirty-seventh, *Pericles,* though not in the Folio, is regarded as canonical. Heminges and Condell suggest in an address "To the great variety of readers" that the republished plays are presented in better form than in the quartos: "Before you were abused with diverse stolen and surreptitious copies, maimed and deformed by the frauds and stealth of injurious impostors that exposed them; even those, are now offered to your view cured and perfect of their limbs, and all the rest absolute in their numbers, as he [i.e., Shakespeare] conceived them."

Whoever was assigned to prepare the texts for publication in the First Folio seems to have taken his job seriously and yet not to have performed it with uniform care. The sources of the texts seem to have been, in general, good unpublished copies or the best published copies. The first play in the collection, *The Tempest,* is divided into acts and scenes, has unusually full stage directions and descriptions of spectacle, and concludes with a list of characters, but the editor was not able (or willing) to present all of the succeeding texts so fully dressed. Later texts occasionally show signs of carelessness: in one scene of *Much Ado About Nothing* the names of actors, instead of characters, appear as speech prefixes, as they had in the quarto, which the Folio reprints; proofreading throughout the Folio is spotty and apparently was done without reference to the printer's copy; the pagination of *Hamlet* jumps from 156 to 257.

A modern editor of Shakespeare must first select his copy; no problem if the play exists only in the Folio, but a considerable problem if the relationship between a quarto and the Folio—or an early quarto and a later one—is unclear. When an editor has chosen what seems to him to be the most authoritative text or texts for his copy, he has not done with making decisions. First of all, he must reckon with Elizabethan spelling. If he is not producing a facsimile, he probably modernizes it, but ought he to preserve the old form of words that apparently were pronounced quite unlike their modern forms—"lanthorn" "alablaster"? If he preserves these forms, is he really preserving Shakespeare's forms or perhaps those of a compositor in the printing house? What is one to do when one finds "lanthorn" and "lantern" in adjacent lines? (The editors of this series in general, but not invariably, assume that words should be spelled in their modern form.) Elizabethan punctuation, too, presents problems. For example in the First Folio, the only text for the play, Macbeth rejects his wife's idea that he can wash the blood from his hand:

> no: this my Hand will rather
> The multitudinous Seas incarnardine,
> Making the Greene one, Red.

Obviously an editor will remove the superfluous capitals, and he will probably alter the spelling to "incarnadine," but will he leave the comma before "red," letting Macbeth speak of the sea as "the green one," or will he (like most modern editors) remove the comma and thus have Macbeth say that his hand will make the ocean *uniformly* red?

An editor will sometimes have to change more than spelling or punctuation. Macbeth says to his wife:

> I dare do all that may become a man,
> Who dares no more, is none.

For two centuries editors have agreed that the second line is unsatisfactory, and have emended "no" to "do": "Who dares do more is none." But when in the same play Ross says that fearful persons

> floate vpon a wilde and violent Sea
> Each way, and moue,

need "move" be emended to "none," as it often is, on the hunch that the compositor misread the manuscript? The editors of the Signet Classic Shakespeare have restrained themselves from making abundant emendations. In their minds they hear Dr. Johnson on the dangers of emending: "I have adopted the Roman sentiment, that it is more honorable to save a citizen than to kill an enemy." Some departures (in addition to spelling, punctuation, and lineation) from the copy text have of course been made, but the original readings are listed in a note following the play, so that the reader can evaluate them for himself.

The editors of the Signet Classic Shakespeare, following tradition, have added line numbers and in many cases act and scene divisions as well as indications of locale at the beginning of scenes. The Folio divided most of the plays into acts and some into scenes. Early eighteenth-century editors increased the divisions. These divisions, which provide a convenient way of referring to passages in the plays, have been retained, but when not in the text chosen as the basis for the Signet Classic text they are enclosed in square brackets [ ] to indicate that they are editorial additions. Similarly, although no play of Shakespeare's published during his lifetime was equipped with indications of locale at the heads of scene divisions, locales have here been added in square brackets for the convenience of the reader, who lacks the information afforded to spectators by costumes, properties, and gestures. The spectator can tell at a glance he is in the throne room, but without an editorial indication the reader may be puzzled for a while. It should be mentioned, incidentally, that there are a few authentic stage directions—perhaps Shakespeare's, perhaps a prompter's—that suggest locales; for example, "Enter Brutus in his orchard," and "They go up into the Senate house." It is hoped that the bracketed additions provide the reader with the sort of help provided in these two authentic directions, but it is equally hoped that the reader will remember that the stage was not loaded with scenery.

No editor during the course of his work can fail to recollect some words Heminges and Condell prefixed to the Folio:

> It had been a thing, we confess, worthy to have been wished, that the author himself had lived to have set forth and overseen his own writings. But since it hath been ordained otherwise, and he by death departed from that right, we pray you do not envy his friends the office of their care and pain to have collected and published them.

Nor can an editor, after he has done his best, forget Heminges and Condell's final words: "And so we leave you to other of his friends, whom if you need can be your guides. If you need them not, you can lead yourselves, and others. And such readers we wish him."

SYLVAN BARNET
Tufts University

Introduction

Love's Labor's Lost is one of Shakespeare's earliest and happiest comedies. It is excellently formed, moving easily towards its conclusion in a masque and a song, at the end recapitulating in all the stage's beauty the courting warfare of the young noblemen and ladies that has made up the chief part of the play, the sparrings and the surrenders and the victories. The play makes the point the theater seems to live to make, that sooner or later love conquers all, and although the title tells us that love's labor is lost, this we know is joking: the happy outcome is certain, and love and long life—as we learn at the end from what G. L. Kittredge called one of the best songs in the world —define the happy prospect.

In this Boccaccio-like setting another comic action plays its part, a comedy about the falsely learned and the grotesquely loving, partly contrasting with and partly parallel to the main story. The king and his lords, moved by the love of philosophy and virtue, have fallen into a most unphilosophical absurdity in supposing that the claims of love can easily be put aside. The foolish scholars light up the folly of the wise ones in still other ways, even as their own courting is mocked by the lovemaking of the others. As in so many of the later plays, it is all there—the multiple plot, the ranging between high and low minds, and love's challenge to every power in the world. All there, and as fluent in its display as in a dance.

The date of the play's composition must be guessed. The 1598 quarto title page mentions a performance of the play before her Highness "this last Christmas," and it adds the phrase, "Newly corrected and augmented."

This, taken along with the evidence of revisions in the text, and with the known dates of certain historical occurrences, leads to pretty substantial arguments for the composition of the play in 1593 or 1594. It should be said, however, that in the past the play was thought to be earlier than this; Coleridge, for example, believed it to be Shakespeare's first play because he thought Shakespeare was bringing into it part of the life he had just left, exploiting his experience as a schoolmaster while the memory of it was still fresh to him. This might push the writing back as far as 1589. More recently Alfred Harbage* has returned to a similar line of reasoning. Likenesses to Lyly's plays in the 1580's and certain considerations making for the possibility that the play was produced by child actors in either a private or public theater, lead him to suggest 1589 or even earlier as the time of performance.

The arguments for a later date point to a general friendliness in England for Henry of Navarre until he reverted to the Church of Rome in July 1593; the beginning of the investigation in 1594 into the atheism of men associated with Sir Walter Raleigh, a group perhaps identified in the play (in IV.iii.254) as "the school of night"; the use of language that suggests the *Venus and Adonis* of 1593, the *Lucrece* of 1594, and sonnets of presumably the same period. And, of course, a number of topical allusions.†

The occasion of the play's first production is not known, but it was surely meant for a private performance —the house of the Earl of Southampton has been suggested—perhaps in 1593. As such it would have been part of festivities in which music and dancing would naturally be called for. The first printed text of the play alludes to a performance before the Queen at Christmas, either in 1597 or 1598, and the play's immediately suc-

---

* *"Love's Labor's Lost* and the Early Shakespeare," *Philological Quarterly*, XLI (1962), 18–36.

† The basic discussion of the play's composition is in Rupert Taylor, *The Date of "Love's Labor's Lost"* (New York: AMS Press, 1966).

ceeding stage history establishes the special suitability of the work for a courtly audience. The substance of the play also makes this clear enough—the initiating idea of learned gentlemen in the company of their monarch retiring from the life of power, the better to perfect their lives; the abjuring the society of women in serious as well as fantastic aspiration, following the directions of the most fashionable writers out of Italy; the mockery of literary men and most particularly of courtiers with ambitions in literature; the battles between the sexes conducted with the most elaborate and sensitive protocol. In large and small matters alike the play seems to be taking something directly out of the life of the court of Elizabeth (wisely enough under another name), making what it takes into something more than life-size. It gives the audience of lords and ladies a mirror in which they will see themselves in all the wit, imagining, beauty and fun they are absorbed in.

The idea of nobility sets the tone for it all. It begins in the king's first speech, it is taken up more than once by the princess, and, ironically, it is finally triumphant in Berowne, the railer at both love and philosophy, so dangerously close in his disposition to the discarding of all values, himself in the end the defender of an aspiration as passionately felt as it is truly thought.

When the king speaks of retiring to the learned academy, we feel the genuine love of learning and of virtue in his words:

> Navarre shall be the wonder of the world;
> Our court shall be a little academe,
> Still and contemplative in living art.

(I.i.12–14)

And the chief critic of the idea is no philistine. He is high-spirited and he is tired of going to school, but he has his wisdom, too, and we judge he has the experience to support it:

> So study evermore is overshot.

> While it doth study to have what it would,
> It doth forget to do the thing it should.

> (I.i.141–43)

And so we immediately perceive that in the conflicts that
are to rage in the play the sparks of thought will be flying
everywhere. The issue is to be granted its proper dignity,
whatever the comic emphasis, and in the end love will
be allowed to break up the academy not only because it
is strong but because it may claim a special worth, and
because the temper of these noble persons is deeply
founded in the cultivation of the best of everything the
world offers.

The princess' first scene gives us so beautiful a picture
of a woman that it carries all before it as if it were the
very praise of womankind. The first words to tell us this
come from one of her lords, advising her on her approach
to the king:

> Be now as prodigal of all dear grace
> As Nature was in making graces dear
> When she did starve the general world beside,
> And prodigally gave them all to you.

> (II.i.9–12)

On the other side, the king is acknowledged as "the sole
inheritor/Of all perfections that a man may owe" (II.i.
5–6). The bounty of the woman and the perfection of the
man, these are the qualities that set the tone, and these
are the persons to lead the dancing interplay, the parry-
ings and the reversals and the resolutions that are to
come. They themselves are the matter of love's labors,
the union of nobility and bounty, like some splendid fore-
shadowing of the masque of Ceres in *The Tempest*.

Nature has its austerity, and love has its temperance,
and the princess' chiding of the busy old lord Boyet for
his flattery is a still more telling criticism of the affectations and grossness of another kind of courtly love—

> my beauty, though but mean,

Needs not the painted flourish of your praise.

(II.i.13–14)

Armado with his affectations brought from Spain and
Italy, and the courtiers with their sonnets, are abusing
"the heart's still rhetoric" (II.i.229). False speaking con-
forms to warped natures, and the play never loses sight
of the idea of inherent excellence in manhood and woman-
hood and of the importance of true expression in love.
Whatever the follies of the great as well as lesser characters, and whatever the ironies whereby nobility and the
taking of oaths are made to seem like tinder before the
fires of love, the decorum of the truly courtly prevails as
the basis of the play's beauty.

The comic ideas also are as alive with intellectuality
as the play's most serious affirmations. When the ladies
call to mind and comment on the lords who accompany
the king—men in the past they had encountered only
briefly—praising them as it appears they deserve to be
praised, we discover that all of them are in love before
they know it. The audience enters into a kind of con-
spiracy with Shakespeare, schooled, as we are certain he
was, by literature and the conventions of the stage, agree-
ing in advance that the great and noble always love the
beautiful, and the beautiful the brave. Since this is the
stage, we know that all these must be paired no matter
what the claims of study. And so, won not only by the
beauty and youth but by the wit of the ladies, we antici-
pate with pleasure the defeat of the men. We have seen
the signs of love in the first words of each of the women
as she sizes up her choice, and while we know enough of
the men to know they will put up a kind of fight, we
cannot be sorry at the prospect of a surrender they themselves will not regret.

The intermingling of the two plots is as expert as the
rest. After the king has announced the program he means
to follow and Berowne has had his say about it, we meet
a clown, Costard, and a fop, Armado. They are showing
off, and Shakespeare mocks both the clown's wenching

and the fop's romancing. The scene is dramatically focussed when the two confront each other in the presence of the one they are both taken with, the country maid, Jaquenetta. Costard, who has been misbehaving, is put into the custody of Armado, who is to guarantee his good behavior. The contrast is in itself pleasing—the fool who from time to time blunders into sense, and the most affected of courtiers who is yet not all fool. And in their folly as in their sense we see that they are being made to pose different versions of the questions the other characters are also asking—what has learning to do with love? and what has love to do with learning? As the plots proceed, the various lovers fall into many absurdities, but the questions themselves continually receive thoughtful answers, or thoughtful mockery. The varieties of the questioning, from such different kinds of lovers, require and get complex and significant answers, and the confusions of Costard and Armado prepare for the resolution Berowne will finally discover.

Meanwhile, the lords about the king are made to show their folly. One after another, subdued to his lady, takes to poetry, and one after another passes across the stage, sonnet in hand, or under his hat, or tucked into his belt—a snow of sonnets. The mockery is so lavish it adds the beauty of a pageant to the absurdity. The noble lords demean themselves in becoming poets, and they glory in their humiliation since they imagine it is pleasing to the ladies. This is indeed what the ladies require of those they favor, but they also require more than words. They require, as Rosaline says of her own lover,

> That he should be my fool, and I his fate.
>
> (V.ii.68)

The play will spell this out. Subjecting themselves to such cruel and whimsical tyrants, the men become as funny as Armado and Moth. Shakespeare lays it on with a trowel—

> To see a king transformèd to a gnat!

> To see great Hercules whipping a gig,
> And profound Solomon to tune a jig,
> And Nestor play at push-pin with the boys,
> And critic Timon laugh at idle toys!
>
> (IV.iii.165–69)

At the end they will endure still greater transformations, but already they are well schooled in the doctrine that love is madness, and that that madness redeems all. As the song jubilantly declares of one lady:

> Thou for whom Jove would swear
> Juno but an Ethiop were.
>
> (IV.iii.116–17)

The beautiful lyric is part of the singing of the whole play, the beauty love worships is the beauty the play is celebrating. All the changes it is ringing on the courting of high and low, on absurdity and exaggeration, on grossness and refinement, are subdued to the grave and splendid beauty that conquers even Jove.

The secondary plot continues the mockery of false ideas of learning and it also brings before us the sight of other kinds of lovemaking. The most obvious point to the mockery of pedantry is as an abuse of what the academy stands for. Holofernes, the walking dictionary, may represent John Florio, or Thomas Harriot. The name Armado brings the Spanish Armada to mind, and so it has been argued that Armado is a portrayal of Sir Walter Raleigh, the man who defeated the Armada. (If this were to be substantiated, it might strengthen the argument of those who think the play was produced shortly after the defeat of the Armada in 1588). Or the character may be thought to represent a quite different person, the arrogant and tedious Gabriel Harvey. Moth may be Thomas Nashe. But however much the possibility of such identifications cause the characters to jump out of their parts, the parts they do play are plainly so much more interesting to the audience for the comments they provide on the characters in the main action. The characters of the minor plot are strangers to the nobility of the others, and in their ambitions and pretensions they are illustrating not only the follies of the court but its essential superiority. The king values learning because it serves the noblest purposes in life; the ideas of the pedants are ignoble. For them it is always the letter at the expense of the spirit, and pride in learning at the expense of its good use.

The point is also being made that the abuse of learning is like the stupidity of affectation in love. The true power of love as well as the true worth of learning is lost upon the low characters, not only in their grossness but in their false refinement too. In the fun Shakespeare is making of them he strikes at everyone, but most of all he means to preserve our esteem for the truer men. They want glory for learning, for the academy, glory that will outlast death, because they want learning to be a light for those who will come after them. It is such men, no mere inkpots, who are love's true targets. In different ways, then, both plots are reinforcing the teaching that love belongs properly to the gentle heart.

Heightening and enrichening this doctrine is the idea of the divinity of love. Character after character speaks of love as if it were a presence as well as a power. The play's title names love as the power at work in the play, and in every turn of the story we are shown events as if they were indeed the manipulations of a god—Eros, although unseen, yet surely directing and effecting all, showing his strength and enforcing his laws. As much as in *All's Well that Ends Well,* those who strive against him strive in vain.

Love's "labor" is a bringing to birth. The remembrances of ancient meetings come fast upon the courtiers and the ladies:

> Did not I dance with you in Brabant once?
> (II.i.114)

and in one after the other the seed burgeons. Part of the poetry as well as the comedy is that this growing of love goes on as it were in isolation. Cutting themselves off from so much of society, from the cares of power as well as from the entanglements with women, the lords are the more defenseless in their idleness. The king himself, treating of the matter the princess has come to negotiate on behalf of her sick father, even as he begins to talk of business finds that his heart is moved. Boyet notes this instantly:

> Why, all his behaviors did make their retire
> To the court of his eye, peeping thorough desire.
> His heart, like an agate with your print impressed,
> Proud with his form, in his eye pride expressed.
>
> (II.i.234–37)

Already love is at work, in the highest as in the lowest, sometimes beautifully and sometimes grotesquely, but always irresistibly.

This leads to the truly inspired idea in the extraordinary, not to say unlikely, happenings presumably only to be accounted for by a god's workings—that all the lovers should from the beginning have had no doubt who were to be their partners. In the masquing, the ladies switched their lords' favors in order to trick their lovers into another perjury, like Portia and Nerissa in *The Merchant of Venice,* merry in forging other chains for their slaves. So this time the lords will swear again, but to the wrong partners—as if another Puck were at work—and the ladies can mock the men until, as Berowne says, they are "dry-beaten" (V.ii.264)—the very blood leaves their faces. They are driven off, and it is no comfort to them to learn finally that they have now forsworn themselves twice. Shakespeare has had his fun with the idea of inexorable destiny in love at first sight, and he makes more fun of it still by asking another question: What is it that love sees?

Love's working and love's presence—a very god— come into full sight in Berowne's great speech, wherein the railer at love and wisdom, himself now enslaved, mocks himself:

> O, and I, forsooth, in love!
> I, that have been love's whip,
> A very beadle to a humorous sigh,

> A critic, nay, a night-watch constable,
> A domineering pedant o'er the boy,
> Than whom no mortal so magnificent!
> This wimpled, whining, purblind, wayward boy,
> This senior-junior, giant-dwarf, Dan Cupid,
> Regent of love rhymes, lord of folded arms,
> Th' anointed sovereign of sighs and groans . . .
> And I to be a corporal of his field!
>
> (III.i.175–89)

To make it worse, he is in love with the one he says is the least beautiful of the ladies, the most wanton, the one who would escape a guardian with a hundred eyes. But he accepts his fate.

> Some men must love my lady, and some Joan.
>
> (III.i.207)

This time Touchstone is a gentleman, and so somewhat more love's fool. But finally he will say more in praise of love than any other will, and however light in touch his words substantiate what the others must now acknowledge:

> From women's eyes this doctrine I derive. . . .
> They are the books, the arts, the academes,
> That show, contain, and nourish all the world;
> Else none at all in aught proves excellent.
>
> (IV.iii.349–53)

With this conclusion the play moves towards its end. The haughty must change their tactics. There is the call to arms and the embrace of battle:

> Advance your standards, and upon them, lords!
>
> (IV.iii.366)

And so they dance, recapitulating in their motions the warring that has made the play, the advances and retreats, the defeats and victories, the strivings, and capitulations, and the final treaties.

For the play's last words there is a song sung by allegorical personages, Spring and Winter, fantastic figures out of the world of musical entertainment and Renaissance allegory. It speaks of flowers and countrymaids and ploughmen, of love and marriage and cuckoldry, of spring and winter, of idleness and of hard work, of nature when it is kind and when it is cruel, of life by the hearth. It is a song about love making peace with life, with things as they are. It provides the most brilliant of comments on all that has been fanciful in the beauty of the play and in the ideas of these fine people. In the perfection and balance of the contrast with all that has gone before, this song sung by the personifications of time is the true culmination of the play, the marriage of sophistication and reality, of the stage and its glory and the strength of love's endurance outside it. The song celebrates the poetry of life as it is, and it is one of Shakespeare's most glorious inspirations that he has it sung by the deities of "curds and flowers," magnificently adorned, without doubt, as the Renaissance imagined gods would be.

The song follows the princess' farewell as she and the ladies leave Navarre, postponing the marriages. The lords are meanwhile to prove themselves by the most strenuous and demanding discipline, for the courtship has been

> A time, methinks, too short,
> To make a world-without-end bargain in.
> (V.ii.789–90)

The words of wisdom are indeed harsh after the music of the god of poetry, as the comment that ends the play says, words that may be given to Armado. They are words that sustain us as the play sustains us, and as the marvelous song does. And the reflection to which the last scene leads us is that love, like learning, is but a part of life, and what the whole of it is there is no one to say—there is only the testing, and good hope.

JOHN ARTHOS
University of Michigan

Love's
Labor's Lost

Ferdinand, King of Navarre
Berowne ⎱
Longaville ⎬ young lords attending on the King
Dumaine ⎰
Boyet, an elderly lord attending on the Princess of France
Marcade, a messenger
Don Adriano de Armado, a fantastical Spaniard
Sir Nathaniel, a curate
Dull, a constable
Holofernes, a schoolmaster
Costard, a clown
Moth, page to Don Armado
A Forester
The Princess of France
Rosaline ⎱
Maria ⎬ ladies attending on the Princess
Katharine ⎰
Jaquenetta, a country wench
Officers and others attendant on the King and Princess

Scene: Navarre]

Love's Labor's Lost

[ACT I

Scene I. *The park of the King of Navarre.*]

Enter Ferdinand King of Navarre, Berowne, Long-
aville, and Dumaine.

King. Let fame, that all hunt after in their lives,
Live regist'red upon our brazen tombs
And then grace us in the disgrace°1 of death,
When, spite of cormorant° devouring time,
Th' endeavor of this present breath may buy   5
That honor which shall bate° his scythe's keen edge
And make us heirs of all eternity.
Therefore, brave conquerors—for so you are
That war against your own affections
And the huge army of the world's desires—   10
Our late edict shall strongly stand in force:
Navarre shall be the wonder of the world;
Our court shall be a little academe,°
Still and contemplative in living art.°

---

1 The degree sign (°) indicates a footnote, which is keyed to the
text by line number. Text references are printed in **boldface** type;
the annotation follows in roman type.   I.i.3 **disgrace** degradation
4 **cormorant** ravenous 6 **bate** make dull 13 **academe** academy
14 **Still . . . art** continually studying the art of living

15 You three, Berowne, Dumaine, and Longaville,
Have sworn for three years' term to live with me,
My fellow scholars, and to keep those statutes
That are recorded in this schedule here.
Your oaths are passed; and now subscribe your
names,
20 That his own hand may strike his honor down
That violates the smallest branch herein.
If you are armed° to do as sworn to do,
Subscribe to your deep oaths, and keep it too.

Longaville. I am resolved. 'Tis but a three years' fast.
25 The mind shall banquet though the body pine.
Fat paunches have lean pates, and dainty bits
Make rich the ribs, but bankrout° quite the wits.

Dumaine. My loving lord, Dumaine is mortified.°
The grosser manner of these world's delights
30 He throws upon the gross world's baser slaves.
To love, to wealth, to pomp, I pine and die,
With all these living in philosophy.

Berowne. I can but say their protestation over°—
So much, dear liege, I have already sworn,
35 That is, to live and study here three years.
But there are other strict observances:
As not to see a woman in that term—
Which I hope well is not enrollèd there;
And one day in a week to touch no food,
40 And but one meal on every day beside—
The which I hope is not enrollèd there;
And then to sleep but three hours in the night,
And not be seen to wink of° all the day
(When I was wont to think no harm all night
45 And make a dark night too of half the day)—
Which I hope well is not enrollèd there.
O, these are barren tasks, too hard to keep,
Not to see ladies, study, fast, not sleep!

22 **armed** resolved   27 **bankrout** bankrupt   28 **mortified** dead to
worldly pleasures   33 **say their protestation over** repeat their solemn
declarations   43 **wink of** close the eyes during

King. Your oath is passed, to pass away from these.

Berowne. Let me say no, my liege, and if° you please.   50
   I only swore to study with your Grace
   And stay here in your court for three years' space.

Longaville. You swore to that, Berowne, and to the
   rest.

Berowne. By yea and nay,° sir, then I swore in jest.
   What is the end of study, let me know?   55

King. Why, that to know which else we should not
   know.

Berowne. Things hid and barred, you mean, from
   common sense?

King. Ay, that is study's godlike recompense.

Berowne. Come on then, I will swear to study so,
   To know the thing I am forbid to know: 60
   As thus—to study where I well may dine
   When I to feast expressly am forbid;
   Or study where to meet some mistress fine
   When mistresses from common sense are hid;
   Or having sworn too hard-a-keeping oath,   65
   Study to break it and not break my troth.°
   If study's gain be thus, and this be so,
   Study knows that which yet it doth not know.
   Swear me to this, and I will ne'er say no.

King. These be the stops° that hinder study quite   70
   And train° our intellects to vain delight.

Berowne. Why, all delights are vain, but that most
   vain
   Which, with pain purchased, doth inherit pain:
   As, painfully to pore upon a book,
   To seek the light of truth, while truth the while   75
   Doth falsely° blind the eyesight of his look.

50 **and if** if   54 **By yea and nay** in all earnestness   66 **troth** faith
70 **stops** obstructions   71 **train** entice   76 **falsely** treacherously

Light seeking light doth light of light beguile;°
So, ere you find where light in darkness lies,
Your light grows dark by losing of your eyes.
80   Study me how to please the eye indeed
By fixing it upon a fairer eye,
Who dazzling so, that eye shall be his heed°
And give him light that it was blinded by.
Study is like the heaven's glorious sun,
85   That will not be deep-searched with saucy looks.
Small have continual plodders ever won
Save base authority from others' books.
These earthly godfathers° of heaven's lights,
That give a name to every fixèd star
90   Have no more profit of their shining nights
Than those that walk and wot° not what they are.
Too much to know is to know nought but fame;°
And every godfather can give a name.

King. How well he's read to reason against reading!

Dumaine. Proceeded° well, to stop all good proceed-
95   ing!

Longaville. He weeds the corn,° and still lets grow the
weeding.°

Berowne. The spring is near, when green geese° are
a-breeding.

Dumaine. How follows that?

Berowne.   Fit in his place and time.

Dumaine. In reason nothing.

Berowne.   Something then in rhyme.

100 *King.* Berowne is like an envious sneaping° frost
That bites the first-born infants of the spring.

---

77 **Light . . . beguile** i.e., eyes in seeking truth lose their sight in too
much seeking   82 **heed** protector   88 **earthly godfathers** i.e., as-
tronomers   91 **wot** know   92 **fame** report   95 **Proceeded** took a
degree at the university   96 **corn** wheat   96 **weeding** weeds   97
green geese geese born the previous autumn   100 **sneaping** nipping
(Berowne's "rhyme" is taken as "rime" or frost)

Berowne. Well, say I am! Why should proud summer
  boast
Before the birds have any cause to sing?
Why should I joy in an abortive birth?
At Christmas I no more desire a rose   *105*
Than wish a snow in May's new-fangled shows,
But like of each thing that in season grows.
So you—to study now it is too late—
Climb o'er the house to unlock the little gate.

King. Well, sit you out. Go home, Berowne. Adieu.   *110*

Berowne. No, my good lord, I have sworn to stay with
  you;
And though I have for barbarism° spoke more
Than for that angel knowledge you can say,
Yet confident I'll keep what I have swore,
And bide the penance of each three years' day.°   *115*
Give me the paper, let me read the same,
And to the strictest decrees I'll write my name.

King. How well this yielding rescues thee from shame!

Berowne. [*Reads*] "Item. That no woman shall come
  within a mile of my court—" Hath this been pro-   *120*
  claimed?

Longaville. Four days ago.

Berowne. Let's see the penalty. [*Reads*] "—on pain of
  losing her tongue." Who devised this penalty?

Longaville. Marry,° that did I.

Berowne.   Sweet lord, and why?   *125*

Longaville. To fright them hence with that dread penalty.

Berowne. A dangerous law against gentility!°
  [*Reads*] "Item. If any man be seen to talk with a
  woman within the term of three years, he shall

112 **barbarism** philistinism   115 **each three years' day** each day of
the three years   125 **Marry** By Mary (mild oath)   127 **gentility**
good manners

130 endure such public shame as the rest of the court
     can possibly devise."
     This article, my liege, yourself must break;
     For well you know here comes in embassy
     The French king's daughter with yourself to speak,
135 A maid of grace and complete majesty,
     About surrender up of Aquitaine
     To her decrepit, sick, and bed-rid father.
     Therefore this article is made in vain,
     Or vainly comes th' admirèd princess hither.

140 *King.* What say you, lords? Why, this was quite forgot.

     Berowne. So study evermore is overshot.°
     While it doth study to have what it would,
     It doth forget to do the thing it should;
     And when it hath the thing it hunteth most,
145 'Tis won as towns with fire°—so won, so lost.

     King. We must of force° dispense with this decree.
     She must lie° here on mere° necessity.

     Berowne. Necessity will make us all forsworn
     Three thousand times within this three years' space:
150 For every man with his affects° is born,
     Not by might mast'red, but by special grace.
     If I break faith, this word shall speak for me,
     I am forsworn "on mere necessity."
     So to the laws at large I write my name;
                              [*Subscribes.*]
155 And he that breaks them in the least degree
     Stands in attainder of° eternal shame.
     Suggestions° are to other as to me,
     But I believe, although I seem so loath,°
     I am the last that will last keep his oath.
160 But is there no quick recreation granted?

     King. Ay, that there is. Our court, you know, is
     haunted

     141 **overshot** wide of the mark   145 **won as towns with fire** destroyed
     in being won   146 **of force** of necessity   147 **lie** lodge   147 **mere**
     simple   150 **affects** passions   156 **in attainder** of to be condemned
     to   157 **Suggestions** temptations   158 **loath** reluctant

With a refinèd traveler of Spain,
A man in all the world's new fashion planted,
That hath a mint of phrases in his brain;
One who the music of his own vain tongue   165
Doth ravish like enchanting harmony;
A man of complements,° whom right and wrong
Have chose as umpire of their mutiny.
This child of fancy, that Armado hight,°
For interim° to our studies shall relate   170
In high-born words the worth of many a knight
From tawny Spain, lost in the world's debate.
How you delight, my lords, I know not, I,
But, I protest, I love to hear him lie,
And I will use him for my minstrelsy.°   175

Berowne. Armado is a most illustrious wight,
A man of fire-new° words, fashion's own knight.

Longaville. Costard the swain° and he shall be our
      sport;
And so to study three years is but short.

      *Enter [Dull,] a Constable, with Costard, [a Clown,]
            with a letter.*

Dull. Which is the duke's own person?   180

Berowne. This, fellow. What wouldst?

Dull. I myself reprehend° his own person, for I am
his Grace's farborough.° But I would see his own
person in flesh and blood.

Berowne. This is he.   185

Dull. Signior Arm—Arm—commends you. There's
villainy abroad. This letter will tell you more.

Costard. Sir, the contempts° thereof are as touching
me.

167 **complements** formal manners 169 **hight** is named 170 **in-
terim** interruption 175 **minstrelsy** court entertainer 177 **fire-new**
fresh from the mint 178 **swain** countryman 182 **reprehend** (Dull
means to say, "represent") 183 **farborough** petty constable
188 **contempts** (Costard means the "contents" of the letter)

190 *King.* A letter from the magnificent Armado.

Berowne. How low soever the matter, I hope in God
for high words.

Longaville. A high hope for a low heaven. God grant
us patience!

195 *Berowne.* To hear, or forbear hearing?

Longaville. To hear meekly, sir, and to laugh moder-
ately, or to forbear both.

Berowne. Well, sir, be it as the style shall give us
cause to climb in the merriness.

200 *Costard.* The matter is to me, sir, as concerning
Jaquenetta. The manner of it is, I was taken with
the manner.°

Berowne. In what manner?

Costard. In manner and form following, sir—all those
205 three: I was seen with her in the manor-house, sitting with her upon the form,° and taken following
her into the park; which, put together, is, in manner and form, following. Now, sir, for the manner—
it is the manner of a man to speak to a woman.
210 For the form—in some form.

Berowne. For the following, sir?

Costard. As it shall follow in my correction,° and
God defend the right!

King. Will you hear this letter with attention?

215 *Berowne.* As we would hear an oracle.

Costard. Such is the simplicity of man to hearken
after the flesh.

King. [*Reads*] "Great deputy, the welkin's vicegerent,°
and sole dominator of Navarre, my soul's earth's
220 God, and body's fost'ring patron—"

201–02 **with the manner** in the act   206 **form** bench   212 **correction**
punishment   218 **welkin's vicegerent** deputy-ruler of heaven

Costard. Not a word of Costard yet.

King. "So it is—"

Costard. It may be so; but if he say it is so, he is, in telling true, but so.°

King. Peace!   225

Costard. Be to me and every man that dares not fight.

King. No words!

Costard. Of other men's secrets, I beseech you.

King. [*Reads*] "So it is, besieged with sable-colored melancholy, I did commend the black-oppressing   230 humor° to the most wholesome physic° of thy health-giving air; and, as I am a gentleman, betook myself to walk. The time When? About the sixth hour; when beasts most graze, birds best peck, and men sit down to that nourishment which is   235 called supper. So much for the time When. Now for the ground Which? Which, I mean, I walked upon. It is ycleped° thy park. Then for the place Where? Where, I mean, I did encounter that obscene and most preposterous event, that draweth   240 from my snow-white pen° the ebon-colored ink, which here thou viewest, beholdest, surveyest, or seest. But to the place Where? It standeth north-north-east and by east from the west corner of thy curious-knotted° garden. There did I see that low-   245 spirited swain, that base minnow of thy mirth—"

Costard. Me?

King. "that unlettered° small-knowing soul—"

Costard. Me?

King. "that shallow vassal°—"   250

---

224 **but so** not worth much   230–31 **black-oppressing humor** fluid
in the body that causes melancholy   231 **physic** treatment   238 **ycleped** called   241 **snow-white pen** goose-quill   245 **curious-knotted**
flower beds and paths in intricate patterns   248 **unlettered** illiterate
250 **vassal** underling

Costard. Still me!

King. "which, as I remember, hight° Costard—"

Costard. O me!

King. "sorted and consorted, contrary to thy estab-
255   lished proclaimed edict and continent canon,°
which with—O, with—but with this I passion to
say wherewith—"

Costard. With a wench.

King. "with a child of our grandmother Eve, a female;
260   or, for thy more sweet understanding, a woman.
Him I (as my ever-esteemed duty pricks° me on)
have sent to thee, to receive the meed° of punishment, by thy sweet Grace's officer, Anthony Dull,
a man of good repute, carriage, bearing, and esti-
265   mation."

Dull. Me, an 't shall please you: I am Anthony Dull.

King. "For Jaquenetta (so is the weaker vessel°
called), which I apprehended with the aforesaid
swain, I keep her as a vessel of thy law's fury, and
270   shall, at the least of thy sweet notice,° bring her
to trial. Thine in all compliments of devoted and
heart-burning heat of duty,
                  Don Adriano de Armado."

Berowne. This is not so well as I looked for, but the
275   best that ever I heard.

King. Ay, the best for the worst. But, sirrah,° what
say you to this?

Costard. Sir, I confess the wench.

King. Did you hear the proclamation?

---

252 **hight** called   255 **continent canon** the decree restraining the
members of the Academy   261 **pricks** spurs   262 **meed** reward
267 **weaker vessel** (general phrase for "womankind")   270 **at the
least . . . notice** at the slightest indication of thy concern   276 **sirrah**
(term of address used to an inferior)

Costard. I do confess much of the hearing it, but little   *280*
of the marking of it.

King. It was proclaimed a year's imprisonment to be
taken with a wench.

Costard. I was taken with none, sir; I was taken with
a damsel.   *285*

King. Well, it was proclaimed "damsel."

Costard. This was no damsel neither, sir, she was a
virgin.

King. It is so varied° too, for it was proclaimed
"virgin."   *290*

Costard. If it were, I deny her virginity. I was taken
with a maid.

King. This maid will not serve your turn, sir.

Costard. This maid will serve my turn,° sir.

King. Sir, I will pronounce your sentence: you shall   *295*
fast a week with bran and water.

Costard. I had rather pray a month with mutton and
porridge.

King. And Don Armado shall be your keeper.
My Lord Berowne, see him delivered o'er.   *300*
And go we, lords, to put in practice that
Which each to other hath so strongly sworn.
          [*Exeunt King, Longaville, and Dumaine.*]

Berowne. I'll lay° my head to any good man's hat,
These oaths and laws will prove an idle scorn.
Sirrah, come on.   *305*

Costard. I suffer for the truth, sir, for true it is I was
taken with Jaquenetta, and Jaquenetta is a true°
girl. And therefore welcome the sour cup of prosperity! Affliction may one day smile again, and till
then sit thee down, sorrow!   *Exeunt.*   *310*

---

289 **varied** distinguished   294 **turn** (Costard uses the word in a
bawdy sense)   303 **lay** bet   307 **true** honest

[Scene II. *The park.*]

Enter Armado and Moth,°　his Page.

Armado. Boy, what sign is it when a man of great
spirit grows melancholy?

Moth. A great sign, sir, that he will look sad.

Armado. Why, sadness is one and the selfsame thing,
5　　dear imp.

Moth. No, no, O Lord, sir, no!

Armado. How canst thou part° sadness and melancholy, my tender juvenal?°

Moth. By a familiar demonstration of the working,
10　　my tough signor.°

Armado. Why tough signor? Why tough signor?

Moth. Why tender juvenal? Why tender juvenal?

Armado. I spoke it, tender juvenal, as a congruent
epitheton° appertaining to thy young days, which
15　　we may nominate tender.

Moth. And I, tough signor, as an appertinent title to
your old time, which we may name tough.

Armado. Pretty and apt.

Moth. How mean you, sir? I pretty, and my saying
20　　apt? Or I apt and my saying pretty?

I.ii.s.d. **Moth** (probably pronounced, and with the meaning of,
"mote," i.e., speck)　7 **part** distinguish between　8 **juvenal** youth
(it may also signify *Juvenal*, the Roman satirist, and allude to the
nickname of Thomas Nashe, Elizabethan writer)　10 **signor** (with
a pun on "senior")　13–14 **congruent epitheton** appropriate ad-
jective

Armado. Thou pretty, because little.

Moth. Little pretty, because little. Wherefore apt?

Armado. And therefore apt because quick.

Moth. Speak you this in my praise, master?

Armado. In thy condign° praise.   25

Moth. I will praise an eel with the same praise.

Armado. What, that an eel is ingenious?

Moth. That an eel is quick.

Armado. I do say thou art quick in answers. Thou heat'st my blood.   30

Moth. I am answered, sir.

Armado. I love not to be crossed.

Moth. [*Aside*] He speaks the mere contrary—crosses° love not him.

Armado. I have promised to study three years with   35
the duke.

Moth. You may do it in an hour, sir.

Armado. Impossible.

Moth. How many is one thrice told?

Armado. I am ill at reck'ning—it fitteth the spirit of   40
a tapster.°

Moth. You are a gentleman and a gamester, sir.

Armado. I confess both. They are both the varnish°
of a complete man.

Moth. Then I am sure you know how much the gross   45
sum of deuce-ace amounts to.

Armado. It doth amount to one more than two.

---

25 **condign** well-deserved   33 **crosses** coins (so named for the crosses engraved on them)   41 **tapster** bartender   43 **varnish** outward gloss

Moth. Which the base vulgar do call three.

Armado. True.

50 *Moth.* Why, sir, is this such a piece of study? Now
here is three studied ere ye'll thrice wink; and how
easy it is to put "years" to the word "three," and
study three years in two words, the dancing horse°
will tell you.

55 *Armado.* A most fine figure.°

Moth. [*Aside*] To prove you a cipher.

Armado. I will hereupon confess I am in love, and
as it is base for a soldier to love, so am I in love
with a base wench. If drawing my sword against
60 the humor° of affection would deliver me from the
reprobate thought of it, I would take Desire pris-
oner and ransom him to any French courtier for
a new devised cursy.° I think scorn° to sigh: methinks I should outswear° Cupid. Comfort me, boy.
65 What great men have been in love?

Moth. Hercules, master.

Armado. Most sweet Hercules! More authority, dear
boy, name more; and, sweet my child, let them
be men of good repute and carriage.

70 *Moth.* Samson, master—he was a man of good carriage, great carriage, for he carried the town-gates
on his back like a porter, and he was in love.

Armado. O well-knit Samson, strong-jointed Samson!
I do excel thee in my rapier as much as thou didst
75 me in carrying gates. I am in love too. Who was
Samson's love, my dear Moth?

Moth. A woman, master.

---

53 **dancing horse** (a performing horse well-known for beating out
numbers) 55 **figure** figure of speech 60 **humor** innate disposition 63 **new devised cursy** novel mannerism 63 **think scorn** dis-
dain 64 **outswear** forswear

Armado. Of what complexion?°

Moth. Of all the four,° or the three, or the two, or
one of the four.   80

Armado. Tell me precisely of what complexion.

Moth. Of the sea-water green, sir.

Armado. Is that one of the four complexions?

Moth. As I have read, sir, and the best of them too.

Armado. Green° indeed is the color of lovers. But to   85
have a love of that color, methinks Samson had
small reason for it. He surely affected her for her
wit.°

Moth. It was so, sir, for she had a green wit.

Armado. My love is most immaculate white and red.   90

Moth. Most maculate° thoughts, master, are masked
under such colors.

Armado. Define, define, well-educated infant.

Moth. My father's wit, and my mother's tongue, assist
me!   95

Armado. Sweet invocation of a child, most pretty and
pathetical.

Moth. If she be made of white and red,
            Her faults will ne'er be known,
        For blushing cheeks by faults are bred,   100
            And fears by pale white shown.
        Then if she fear or be to blame,
            By this you shall not know,
        For still her cheeks possess the same
            Which native° she doth owe.°   105
    A dangerous rhyme, master, against the reason of
    white and red.

78 **complexion** disposition   79 **all the four** (the four humors or
fluids of the body: blood, phlegm, bile, black bile)   85 **Green** (im-
mature)   88 **wit** mind   91 **maculate** spotted   105 **native** by nature
105 **owe** possess

Armado. Is there not a ballet,° boy, of the King and
    the Beggar?

110 *Moth.* The world was very guilty of such a ballet
    some three ages since. But I think now 'tis not to
    be found, or if it were, it would neither serve for
    the writing nor the tune.

Armado. I will have that subject newly writ o'er, that
115   I may example my digression° by some mighty
    precedent. Boy, I do love that country girl that I
    took in the park with the rational hind,° Costard.
    She deserves well.

Moth. [*Aside*] To be whipped—and yet a better love
120   than my master.

Armado. Sing, boy. My spirit grows heavy in love.

Moth. And that's great marvel, loving a light wench.

Armado. I say, sing.

Moth. Forbear till this company be past.

        Enter [Costard, the] Clown, [Dull, the]
        Constable, and [Jaquenetta, a] Wench.

125 *Dull.* Sir, the duke's pleasure is that you keep Costard
    safe, and you must suffer him to take no delight
    nor no penance,° but 'a° must fast three days a
    week. For this damsel, I must keep her at the park
    —she is allowed for the day-woman.° Fare you
130   well.

Armado. I do betray myself with blushing. Maid!

Jaquenetta. Man?

Armado. I will visit thee at the lodge.

Jaquenetta. That's hereby.

---

108 **ballet** ballad   115 **digression** (Armado means to say, "transgression")   117 **rational hind** intelligent yokel   127 **penance** (perhaps Dull means to say "pleasance," meaning pleasure)   127 **'a** he
129 **allowed for the day-woman** admitted as the dairy maid

Armado. I know where it is situate.

Jaquenetta. Lord, how wise you are!

Armado. I will tell thee wonders.

Jaquenetta. With that face?

Armado. I love thee.

Jaquenetta. So I heard you say.   140

Armado. And so farewell.

Jaquenetta. Fair weather after you!

Dull. Come, Jaquenetta, away!

> *Exeunt [Dull and Jaquenetta].*

Armado. Villain, thou shalt fast for thy offenses ere
  thou be pardoned.   145

Costard. Well, sir, I hope when I do it I shall do it
  on a full stomach.°

Armado. Thou shalt be heavily punished.

Costard. I am more bound to you than your fellows,°
  for they are but lightly rewarded.   150

Armado. Take away this villain. Shut him up.

Moth. Come, you transgressing slave, away!

Costard. Let me not be pent up, sir. I will fast, being
  loose.

Moth. No, sir, that were fast and loose.° Thou shalt   155
  to prison.

Costard. Well, if ever I do see the merry days of desolation that I have seen, some shall see.

Moth. What shall some see?

Costard. Nay, nothing, Master Moth, but what they   160
  look upon. It is not for prisoners to be too silent

---

147 **on a full stomach** bravely   149 **fellows** servants   155 **fast and
loose** not playing fairly

in their words,° and therefore I will say nothing. I
thank God I have as little patience as another man,
and therefore I can be quiet.   *Exit [with Moth].*

165 *Armado.* I do affect° the very ground (which is base)
where her shoe (which is baser) guided by her foot
(which is basest) doth tread. I shall be forsworn
(which is a great argument of falsehood) if I love.
And how can that be true love which is falsely at-
170 tempted? Love is a familiar;° Love is a devil. There
is no evil angel but Love. Yet was Samson so
tempted, and he had an excellent strength; yet was
Solomon so seduced, and he had a very good wit.
Cupid's butt-shaft° is too hard for Hercules' club,
175 and therefore too much odds for a Spaniard's
rapier. The first and second cause° will not serve
my turn; the *passado*° he respects not, the *duello*°
he regards not. His disgrace is to be called boy, but
his glory is to subdue men. Adieu, valor; rust, ra-
180 pier; be still, drum; for your manager is in love;
yea, he loveth. Assist me some extemporal god of
rhyme,° for I am sure I shall turn sonnet.° Devise,
wit; write, pen; for I am for whole volumes in folio.
                                        Exit.

162 **words** (probably with pun on wards = cells)   165 **affect** love
170 **familiar** attendant spirit   174 **butt-shaft** unbarbed   arrow
176 **first and second cause** (referring to rules governing the conduct
of a duel)   177 **passado** forward thrust   177 **duello** correct way
of dueling   181–82 **extemporal god of rhyme** god of rhymes written on the spur of the moment   182 **turn sonnet** compose a sonnet

[ACT II

Scene I. *The park.*]

Enter the Princess of France, with three attending Ladies [Maria, Katharine, Rosaline] and three Lords, [one named Boyet].

Boyet. Now, madam, summon up your dearest
    spirits.°
  Consider who the king your father sends,
  To whom he sends, and what's his embassy:
  Yourself, held precious in the world's esteem,
  To parley with the sole inheritor°   5
  Of all perfections that a man may owe,°
  Matchless Navarre; the plea of no less weight
  Than Aquitaine, a dowry for a queen.
  Be now as prodigal of all dear grace
  As Nature was in making graces dear°   10
  When she did starve the general world beside,
  And prodigally gave them all to you.

Princess. Good Lord Boyet, my beauty, though but
    mean,
  Needs not the painted flourish° of your praise.
  Beauty is bought by judgment of the eye,   15
  Not utt'red by base sale of chapmen's tongues.°

II.i.1 **dearest spirits** best intelligence 5 **inheritor** possessor 6 **owe** own 10 **graces dear** beauty scarce 14 **painted flourish** elaborate ornament 16 **utt'red ... tongues** put up for sale by hucksters

I am less proud to hear you tell my worth
Than you much willing to be counted wise
In spending your wit in the praise of mine.
20 But now to task the tasker:° good Boyet,
You are not ignorant all-telling fame
Doth noise abroad Navarre hath made a vow,
Till painful study shall outwear three years,
No woman may approach his silent court.
25 Therefore to's seemeth it a needful course,
Before we enter his forbidden gates,
To know his pleasure; and in that behalf,
Bold of your worthiness,° we single you
As our best-moving° fair solicitor.
30 Tell him the daughter of the king of France,
On serious business, craving quick dispatch,
Importunes personal conference with his Grace.
Haste, signify so much while we attend
Like humble-visaged suitors his high will.

35 *Boyet.* Proud of employment, willingly I go.
Exit Boyet.

Princess. All pride is willing pride, and yours is so.
Who are the votaries,° my loving lords,
That are vow-fellows with this virtuous duke?

Lord. Longaville is one.

Princess.   Know you the man?

40 *Maria.* I know him, madam. At a marriage feast
Between Lord Perigort and the beauteous heir
Of Jacques Falconbridge solemnizèd
In Normandy saw I this Longaville.
A man of sovereign parts° he is esteemed,
45 Well fitted in arts, glorious in arms.
Nothing becomes him ill that he would well.°
The only soil of his fair virtue's gloss—

20 **task the tasker** set a task to the one who sets tasks 28 **Bold of
your worthiness** confident of your worth 29 **best-moving** most
persuasive 37 **votaries** those who have sworn a vow 44 **sovereign
parts** lordly qualities 46 **Nothing . . . well** nothing that he values
is unbecoming to him

If virtue's gloss will stain with any soil—
Is a sharp wit matched with too blunt a will,
Whose edge hath power to cut, whose will still wills 50
It should none spare that come within his power.

Princess. Some merry mocking lord, belike—is 't so?

Maria. They say so most that most his humors know.

Princess. Such short-lived wits do wither as they grow.
Who are the rest?   55

Katharine. The young Dumaine, a well-accomplished
    youth,
Of all that virtue love for virtue loved;
Most power to do most harm, least knowing ill,
For he hath wit to make an ill shape good,
And shape to win grace though he had no wit.   60
I saw him at the Duke Alençon's once;
And much too little° of that good I saw
Is my report to° his great worthiness.

Rosaline. Another of these students at that time
Was there with him, if I have heard a truth.   65
Berowne they call him; but a merrier man,
Within the limit of becoming mirth,
I never spent an hour's talk withal.°
His eye begets occasion° for his wit;
For every object that the one doth catch   70
The other turns to a mirth-moving jest,
Which his fair tongue (conceit's expositor°)
Delivers in such apt and gracious words,
That agèd ears play truant at his tales,
And younger hearings are quite ravishèd,   75
So sweet and voluble is his discourse.

Princess. God bless my ladies! Are they all in love,
That every one her own hath garnishèd
With such bedecking ornaments of praise?

---

62 **much too little** far short   63 **to** compared to   68 **withal** with
69 **begets occasion** finds opportunity   72 **conceit's expositor** one
who explains an ingenious notion

Lord. Here comes Boyet.

Enter Boyet.

80 *Princess.*   Now, what admittance,° lord?

Boyet. Navarre had notice of your fair approach;
And he and his competitors° in oath
Were all addressed° to meet you, gentle lady,
Before I came. Marry, thus much I have learnt;
85 He rather means to lodge you in the field,
Like one that comes here to besiege his court,
Than seek a dispensation for his oath
To let you enter his unpeopled house.
                    [*The Ladies mask.*]

Enter Navarre, Longaville, Dumaine, and
Berowne, [*with Attendants*].

Here comes Navarre.

90 *King.* Fair princess, welcome to the court of Navarre.

Princess. "Fair" I give you back again; and "welcome" I have not yet. The roof of this court is too
high to be yours, and welcome to the wide fields
too base to be mine.

95 *King.* You shall be welcome, madam, to my court.

Princess. I will be welcome, then. Conduct me thither.

King. Hear me, dear lady—I have sworn an oath.

Princess. Our Lady help my lord! He'll be forsworn.

King. Not for the world, fair madam, by my will.

Princess. Why, will shall break it, will, and nothing
100   else.

King. Your ladyship is ignorant what it is.

---

80 **admittance** permission to enter   82 **competitors** partners   83 **ad-
dressed** ready

Princess. Were my lord so, his ignorance were wise,
　Where now his knowledge must prove ignorance.
　I hear your Grace hath sworn out house-keeping.°
　'Tis deadly sin to keep that oath, my lord,   105
　And sin to break it.
　But pardon me, I am too sudden-bold;
　To teach a teacher ill beseemeth me.
　Vouchsafe to read the purpose of my coming,
　And suddenly resolve me° in my suit.   110
　　　　　　　　　　　　　　　[Gives a paper.]

King. Madam, I will, if suddenly I may.

Princess. You will the sooner that I were away,
　For you'll prove perjured if you make me stay.

Berowne. Did not I dance with you in Brabant once?

Rosaline. Did not I dance with you in Brabant once?   115

Berowne. I know you did.

Rosaline.　　　　　　　　　　How needless was it then
　To ask the question!

Berowne.　　　　　　　　You must not be so quick.

Rosaline. 'Tis long° of you that spur me with such
　questions.

Berowne. Your wit's too hot, it speeds too fast, 'twill
　tire.

Rosaline. Not till it leave the rider in the mire.   120

Berowne. What time o' day?

Rosaline. The hour that fools should ask.

Berowne. Now fair befall° your mask!

Rosaline. Fair fall the face it covers!

Berowne. And send you many lovers!   125

---

104 **sworn out house-keeping** sworn not to keep house or offer hospitality　110 **suddenly resolve me** quickly give me a decision
118 **long** because　123 **fair befall** good luck to

Rosaline. Amen, so you be none.

Berowne. Nay, then will I be gone.

King. Madam, your father here doth intimate°
The payment of a hundred thousand crowns,
130 Being but the one half of an entire sum
Disbursèd by my father in his wars.
But say that he, or we (as neither have),
Received that sum, yet there remains unpaid
A hundred thousand more, in surety of the which,
135 One part of Aquitaine is bound to us,
Although not valued to the money's worth.
If then the king your father will restore
But that one half which is unsatisfied,
We will give up our right in Aquitaine,
140 And hold fair friendship with his Majesty.
But that, it seems, he little purposeth,
For here he doth demand to have repaid
A hundred thousand crowns; and not demands,
On payment of a hundred thousand crowns,
145 To have his title live in Aquitaine;
Which we much rather had depart withal,°
And have the money by our father lent,
Than Aquitaine, so gelded° as it is.
Dear princess, were not his requests so far
150 From reason's yielding, your fair self should make
A yielding 'gainst some reason in my breast,
And go well satisfied to France again.

Princess. You do the king my father too much wrong,
And wrong the reputation of your name,
155 In so unseeming° to confess receipt
Of that which hath so faithfully been paid.

King. I do protest I never heard of it;
And if you prove it, I'll repay it back
Or yield up Aquitaine.

---

128 **intimate** make known 146 **depart withal** give up 148 **gelded**
cut up 155 **unseeming** not appearing

Princess.   We arrest your word.°
  Boyet, you can produce acquittances°   160
  For such a sum from special officers
  Of Charles his father.

King.   Satisfy me so.

Boyet. So please your Grace, the packet° is not come
  Where that and other specialties° are bound.
  Tomorrow you shall have a sight of them.   165

King. It shall suffice me—at which interview
  All liberal reason I will yield unto.
  Meantime, receive such welcome at my hand
  As honor (without breach of honor) may
  Make tender of° to thy true worthiness.   170
  You may not come, fair princess, within my gates;
  But here without you shall be so received
  As you shall deem yourself lodged in my heart,
  Though so denied fair harbor in my house.
  Your own good thoughts excuse me, and farewell. 175
  Tomorrow shall we visit you again.

Princess. Sweet health and fair desires consort° your
  Grace.

King. Thy own wish wish I thee in every place.
                    Exit [King and his Train].

Berowne. Lady, I will commend you to mine own
  heart.   180

Rosaline. Pray you, do my commendations, I would
  be glad to see it.

Berowne. I would you heard it groan.

Rosaline. Is the fool sick?

Berowne. Sick at the heart.   185

Rosaline. Alack, let it blood!°

---

159 **arrest your word** take your word as security   160 **acquittances**
receipts   163 **packet** package   164 **specialties** particular legal documents   170 **Make tender of** offer   177 **consort** accompany   186 **let
it blood** bleed him

Berowne. Would that do it good?

Rosaline. My physic says ay.

Berowne. Will you prick 't with your eye?

190 *Rosaline.* No point,° with my knife.

Berowne. Now, God save thy life!

Rosaline. And yours from long living!

Berowne. I cannot stay thanksgiving.°   *Exit.*

Enter Dumaine.

Dumaine, Sir, I pray you a word. What lady is that
     same?

195 *Boyet.* The heir of Alençon, Katharine her name.

Dumaine. A gallant lady. Monsieur, fare you well.
                                                  Exit.

[Enter Longaville.]

Longaville. I beseech you a word. What is she in the
     white?

Boyet. A woman sometimes, and° you saw her in the
     light.

Longaville. Perchance light in the light.° I desire her
     name.

Boyet. She hath but one for herself. To desire that
200   were a shame.

Longaville. Pray you, sir, whose daughter?

Boyet. Her mother's, I have heard.

Longaville. God's blessing on your beard!

---

190 **No point** not at all   193 **stay thanksgiving** stay long enough to
give you proper thanks (for your unkind remark)   198 **and** if
199 **light in the light** wanton if rightly perceived

Boyet. Good sir, be not offended.
  She is an heir of Falconbridge.   205

Longaville. Nay, my choler° is ended.
  She is a most sweet lady.

Boyet. Not unlike, sir; that may be.
                          Exit Longaville.

                Enter Berowne.

Berowne. What's her name in the cap?

Boyet. Rosaline, by good hap.   210

Berowne. Is she wedded or no?

Boyet. To her will, sir, or so.°

Berowne. O, you are welcome, sir! Adieu.

Boyet. Farewell to me, sir, and welcome to you.
                          Exit Berowne.

Maria. That last is Berowne, the merry madcap lord. 215
  Not a word with him but a jest.

Boyet.   And every jest but a word.

Princess. It was well done of you to take him at his
  word.

Boyet. I was as willing to grapple as he was to board.

Katharine. Two hot sheeps, marry!

Boyet.   And wherefore not ships?
  No sheep, sweet lamb, unless we feed on your lips. 220

Katharine. You sheep, and I pasture. Shall that finish
  the jest?

Boyet. So you grant pasture for me.
                          [Offers to kiss her.]

206 **choler** wrath   212 **or so** something like that

Katharine.   Not so, gentle beast.
　　My lips are no common,° though several° they be.

Boyet. Belonging to whom?

Katharine.   To my fortunes and me.

Princess. Good wits will be jangling; but, gentles,
225　　agree.
　　This civil war of wits were much better used
　　On Navarre and his book-men, for here 'tis abused.

Boyet. If my observation (which very seldom lies)
　　By the heart's still rhetoric disclosèd with eyes
230　　Deceive me not now, Navarre is infected.

Princess. With what?

Boyet. With that which we lovers entitle "affected."°

Princess. Your reason?

Boyet. Why, all his behaviors° did make their retire
235　　To the court° of his eye, peeping thorough desire.
　　His heart, like an agate° with your print im-
　　　　pressed,°
　　Proud with his form, in his eye pride expressed.
　　His tongue, all impatient to speak and not see,°
　　Did stumble with haste in his eyesight to be;
240　　All senses to that sense did make their repair,
　　To feel only looking on fairest of fair.°
　　Methought all his senses were locked in his eye,
　　As jewels in crystal for some prince to buy;
　　Who, tend'ring° their own worth from where they
　　　　were glassed,°
245　　Did point° you to buy them, along as you passed.

---

223 **no common** i.e., not like pasture held in common   223 **several**
two (the word also, in this context, signifies "private property")
232 **affected** impassioned   234 **behaviors** expression of his feelings
235 **court** watch-post   236 **agate** (stone used for the engraving of
images)   236 **impressed** imprinted   238 **His tongue . . . see** his
tongue, vexed at having the power of speaking without having the
power of seeing   241 **To feel . . . fair** (sight is translated into feeling
in regarding her)   244 **tend'ring** offering   244 **glassed** enclosed in
glass   245 **point** urge

His face's own margent did quote such amazes
That all eyes saw his eyes enchanted with gazes.°
I'll give you Aquitaine, and all that is his,
And° you give him for my sake but one loving kiss.

Princess. Come to our pavilion. Boyet is disposed.　　250

Boyet. But to speak that in words which his eye hath
　disclosed.
I only have made a mouth of his eye
By adding a tongue which I know will not lie.

Rosaline. Thou art an old love-monger, and speakest
　skillfully.

Maria. He is Cupid's grandfather, and learns news of
　him.　　255

Katharine. Then was Venus like her mother, for her
　father is but grim.

Boyet. Do you hear, my mad wenches?

Rosaline.　　　　　　　No.

Boyet.　　　　　　　What then? Do you see?

Rosaline. Ay, our way to be gone.

Boyet.　　　　　　　You are too hard for me.
　　　　　　　　　　Exeunt omnes.°

246–47 **His face's . . . gazes** i.e., the amazement in Navarre's face
drew attention, like comments in a book's margin, to the love in his
eyes　249 **And** if　258 s.d. **omnes** all (Latin)

[ACT III

Scene I. *The park*.]

Enter [Armado, the] Braggart, and [Moth,] his Boy.

Armado. Warble, child, make passionate my sense of
    hearing.

Moth. [*Sings*] Concolinel.°

Armado. Sweet air! Go, tenderness of years,° take
5   this key, give enlargement° to the swain, bring him
    festinately° hither. I must employ him in a letter
    to my love.

Moth. Master, will you win your love with a French
    brawl?°

10 *Armado.* How meanest thou? Brawling in French?

Moth. No, my complete master; but to jig off a tune
    at the tongue's end, canary to it° with your feet,
    humor it with turning up your eyelids, sigh a note
    and sing a note, sometime through the throat as if
15 you swallowed love with singing love, sometime
    through the nose as if you snuffed up love by smell-
    ing love, with your hat penthouse-like o'er the shop

III.i.3 **Concolinel** (perhaps the name of a song)   4 **tenderness of
years** (affected talk for "young fellow")   5 **enlargement** freedom
6 **festinately** quickly   8–9 **French brawl** French dance   12 **canary
to it** dance in a lively way

66

of your eyes, with your arms crossed° on your
thin-belly doublet° like a rabbit on a spit, or your
hands in your pocket like a man after the old paint-   20
ing; and keep not too long in one tune, but a snip°
and away. These are complements,° these are humors, these betray nice wenches (that would be
betrayed without these), and make them men of
note—do you note me?—that most are affected   25
to° these.

Armado. How hast thou purchased this experience?

Moth. By my penny of observation.

Armado. But O—but O—

Moth. "The hobby-horse is forgot."°   30

Armado. Call'st thou my love "hobby-horse"?

Moth. No, master. The hobby-horse is but a colt, and
your love perhaps a hackney.° But have you forgot your love?

Armado. Almost I had.   35

Moth. Negligent student, learn her by heart.

Armado. By heart, and in heart, boy.

Moth. And out of heart, master. All those three I will
prove.

Armado. What wilt thou prove?   40

Moth. A man, if I live; and this, by, in, and without,
upon the instant. By heart you love her, because
your heart cannot come by her; in heart you love
her, because your heart is in love with her; and
out of heart you love her, being out of heart that   45
you cannot enjoy her.

18 **arms crossed** (a sign of melancholy)   19 **thin-belly doublet**
garment unpadded in the lower part (across your thin belly)   21 **snip**
snatch   22 **complements** accompaniments   25–26 **affected to** taken
with   30 **"The hobby-horse is forgot"** (perhaps a phrase from an
old song)   32–33 **hobby-horse, colt, hackney** (slang words for
"whore")

Armado. I am all these three.

Moth. [*Aside*] And three times as much more, and yet nothing at all.

50 *Armado.* Fetch hither the swain. He must carry me a letter.

Moth. A message well sympathized°—a horse to be ambassador for an ass.

Armado. Ha, ha, what sayest thou?

55 *Moth.* Marry, sir, you must send the ass upon the horse, for he is very slow-gaited. But I go.

Armado. The way is but short. Away!

Moth. As swift as lead, sir.

Armado. The meaning, pretty ingenious?
60 Is not lead a metal heavy, dull, and slow?

Moth. Minime,° honest master; or rather, master, no.

Armado. I say, lead is slow.

Moth.   You are too swift, sir, to say so.
Is that lead slow which is fired from a gun?

Armado. Sweet smoke of rhetoric!
65 He reputes me a cannon; and the bullet, that's he:
I shoot thee at the swain.

Moth.   Thump, then, and I flee.
[*Exit.*]

Armado. A most acute juvenal,° voluble and free of grace!
By thy favor, sweet welkin,° I must sigh in thy face:
Most rude melancholy, valor gives thee place.°
70 My herald is returned.

---

52 well sympathized in proper accord 61 Minime by no means
(Latin) 67 juvenal (in two senses) young fellow, satirist 68 welkin
heaven 69 gives thee place gives place to you

Enter [Moth, the] Page and [Costard, the] Clown.

Moth. A wonder, master! Here's a costard° broken
 in a shin.

Armado. Some enigma, some riddle. Come, thy
 l'envoy°—begin.

Costard. No egma, no riddle, no l'envoy; no salve°
 in the mail,° sir. O, sir, plantain,° a plain plantain.
 No l'envoy, no l'envoy, no salve, sir, but a plantain. *73*

Armado. By virtue, thou enforcest laughter; thy silly
 thought, my spleen;° the heaving of my lungs pro-
 vokes me to ridiculous smiling. O, pardon me, my
 stars! Doth the inconsiderate° take salve for
 l'envoy, and the word l'envoy for a salve? *80*

Moth. Do the wise think them other? Is not l'envoy
 a salve?

Armado. No, page; it is an epilogue, or discourse to
 make plain
 Some obscure precedence° that hath tofore been
 sain.°
 I will example it: *85*
   The fox, the ape, and the humble-bee
   Were still at odds, being but three.
 There's the moral. Now the l'envoy.

Moth. I will add the l'envoy. Say the moral again.

Armado. The fox, the ape, and the humble-bee *90*
   Were still at odds, being but three.

Moth. Until the goose came out of door,
   And stayed the odds by adding four.°

---

71 **costard** apple, or head 72 **l'envoy** words ending a composition
by way of leave-taking 73 **salve** (with a pun on *salve*, the Latin
word for salute) 74 **mail** bag, container 74 **plantain** tree whose
leaves were used for healing 77 **spleen** mirth 79 **inconsiderate**
unthinking 84 **precedence** preceding statement 84 **tofore been
sain** been said before 93 **stayed . . . four** turned them into evens
by adding a fourth

Now will I begin your moral, and do you follow
95   with my l'envoy.

   The fox, the ape, and the humble-bee
   Were still at odds, being but three.

Armado. Until the goose came out of door,
   Staying the odds by adding four.

100 *Moth.* A good l'envoy, ending in the goose. Would
you desire more?

Costard. The boy hath sold him a bargain,° a goose
—that's flat.
Sir, your pennyworth is good, and° your goose be
fat.
To sell a bargain well is as cunning as fast and
loose.°
105 Let me see: a fat l'envoy—ay, that's a fat goose.

Armado. Come hither, come hither. How did this
argument begin?

Moth. By saying that a costard was broken in a shin.
Then called you for the l'envoy.

Costard. True, and I for a plantain; thus came your
argument in;
Then the boy's fat l'envoy, the goose that you
110 bought,
And he ended the market.

Armado. But tell me, how was there a costard broken
in a shin?

Moth. I will tell you sensibly.°

115 *Costard.* Thou hast no feeling of it, Moth. I will speak
that l'envoy:
I, Costard, running out, that was safely within,
Fell over the threshold and broke my shin.

Armado. We will talk no more of this matter.

120 *Costard.* Till there be more matter° in the shin.

102 **sold him a bargain** made a fool of him 103 **and** if 104 **fast and loose** cheating 114 **sensibly** with feeling 120 **matter** pus

Armado. Sirrah Costard, I will enfranchise° thee.

Costard. O, marry me to one Frances! I smell some
l'envoy, some goose, in this.

Armado. By my sweet soul, I mean setting thee at
liberty, enfreedoming thy person. Thou wert im- 125
mured, restrained, captivated, bound.

Costard. True, true, and now you will be my purga-
tion and let me loose.

Armado. I give thee thy liberty, set thee from dur-
ance, and in lieu thereof, impose on thee nothing 130
but this. [*Gives a letter.*] Bear this significant° to
the country maid Jaquenetta. [*Gives a coin.*] There
is remuneration; for the best ward° of mine honor
is rewarding my dependents. Moth, follow.

Moth. Like the sequel, I. Signior Costard, adieu. 135
                    Exit [*Armado, followed by Moth*].

Costard. My sweet ounce of man's flesh, my incony°
Jew!—Now will I look to his remuneration. Remuneration? O that's the Latin word for three farthings. Three farthings—remuneration. "What's the
price of this inkle?"° "One penny." "No, I'll give 140
you a remuneration." Why, it carries it! Remuneration! Why, it is a fairer name than French
crown.° I will never buy and sell out of this word.

                    Enter Berowne.

Berowne. O my good knave Costard, exceedingly well
met.   145

Costard. Pray you, sir, how much carnation° ribbon
may a man buy for a remuneration?

Berowne. O, what is a remuneration?

---

121 **enfranchise** set free   131 **significant** letter   133 **ward** protection
136 **incony** darling   140 **inkle** band of linen   142–43 **French crown**
(in two senses: a coin, and the baldness caused by syphilis, the so-
called "French disease")   146 **carnation** flesh-colored

Costard. Marry, sir, halfpenny farthing.

150 *Berowne.* O, why then, three-farthing-worth of silk.

Costard. I thank your worship. God be wi' you!

Berowne. O stay, slave, I must employ thee.
As thou wilt win my favor, good my knave,
Do one thing for me that I shall entreat.

155 *Costard.* When would you have it done, sir?

Berowne. O, this afternoon.

Costard. Well, I will do it, sir. Fare you well.

Berowne. O, thou knowest not what it is.

Costard. I shall know, sir, when I have done it.

160 *Berowne.* Why, villain, thou must know first.

Costard. I will come to your worship tomorrow morning.

Berowne. It must be done this afternoon. Hark, slave,
it is but this:
165 The princess comes to hunt here in the park,
And in her train there is a gentle lady;
When tongues speak sweetly, then they name her name,
And Rosaline they call her. Ask for her,
And to her white hand see thou do commend
This sealed-up counsel. [*Gives him a letter and a*
170 *shilling.*] There's thy guerdon.° Go.

Costard. Gardon, O sweet gardon! Better than remuneration—a 'leven-pence farthing better. Most
sweet gardon! I will do it, sir, in print.° Gardon!
Remuneration!   *Exit.*

175 *Berowne.* O, and I, forsooth, in love!
I, that have been love's whip,
A very beadle° to a humorous sigh,

---

170 **guerdon** reward   173 **in print** most carefully   177 **beadle** parish constable

A critic, nay, a night-watch constable,
A domineering pedant o'er the boy,
Than whom no mortal so magnificent!   180
This wimpled,° whining, purblind,° wayward boy,
This senior-junior, giant-dwarf, Dan° Cupid,
Regent of love-rhymes, lord of folded arms,
Th' anointed sovereign of sighs and groans,
Liege° of all loiterers and malcontents,   185
Dread prince of plackets,° king of codpieces,°
Sole imperator and great general
Of trotting paritors°—O my little heart!—
And I to be a corporal of his field,°
And wear his colors like a tumbler's° hoop!   190
What? I love? I sue? I seek a wife?
A woman that is like a German clock,
Still a-repairing, ever out of frame,°
And never going aright, being a watch,
But being watched that it may still go right!   195
Nay, to be perjured, which is worst of all;
And, among three, to love the worst of all,
A whitely° wanton with a velvet brow,
With two pitch balls stuck in her face for eyes.
Ay, and, by heaven, one that will do the deed,°   200
Though Argus° were her eunuch and her guard!
And I to sigh for her, to watch for her,
To pray for her! Go to, it is a plague
That Cupid will impose for my neglect
Of his almighty dreadful little might.   205
Well, I will love, write, sigh, pray, sue, groan.
Some men must love my lady, and some Joan.
                                          [*Exit.*]

---

181 **wimpled** covered with a muffler   181 **purblind** completely blind
182 **Dan** ("don," a derivation of *dominus,* lord)   185 **Liege** lord
186 **plackets** slits in petticoats (vulgar term for women)   186 **codpieces** cloth covering the opening in men's breeches   188 **paritors**
(officers of the Ecclesiastical Court who serve summonses for certain, often sexual, offenses)   189 **corporal of his field** aide to a
general   190 **tumbler's** acrobat's   193 **frame** order   198 **whitely**
pale   200 **do the deed** perform the act of coition   201 **Argus** (ancient mythological being with a hundred eyes)

[ACT IV

Scene I. *The park.*]

Enter the Princess, a Forester, her Ladies,
and her Lords.

Princess. Was that the king, that spurred his horse so
  hard
  Against the steep uprising of the hill?

Forester. I know not, but I think it was not he.

Princess. Whoe'er 'a° was, 'a showed a mounting
  mind.°
5   Well, lords, today we shall have our dispatch;
  On Saturday we will return to France.
  Then, forester, my friend, where is the bush
  That we must stand and play the murderer in?

Forester. Hereby, upon the edge of yonder coppice,°
10 A stand where you may make the fairest shoot.

Princess. I thank my beauty, I am fair that shoot,
  And thereupon thou speak'st the fairest shoot.

Forester. Pardon me, madam, for I meant not so.

Princess. What, what? First praise me, and again say
  no?
15 O short-lived pride! Not fair? Alack for woe!

Forester. Yes, madam, fair.

IV.i.4 'a he   4 **mounting mind** lofty spirit (with pun on "mountain")
9 **coppice** undergrowth of small trees

74

Princess.   Nay, never paint° me now!
Where fair is not, praise cannot mend the brow.°
Here, good my glass,° take this for telling true—
                              [*giving him money*]
Fair payment for foul words is more than due.

Forester. Nothing but fair is that which you inherit.   20

Princess. See, see—my beauty will be saved by
  merit!°
O heresy in fair,° fit for these days!
A giving hand, though foul, shall have fair praise.
But come, the bow! Now mercy goes to kill,°
And shooting well is then accounted ill.   25
Thus will I save my credit in the shoot:
Not wounding, pity would not let me do 't;
If wounding, then it was to show my skill,
That more for praise than purpose meant to kill.
And out of question so it is sometimes,   30
Glory° grows guilty of detested crimes,
When, for fame's sake, for praise, an outward part,
We bend to that the working of the heart;
As I for praise alone now seek to spill
The poor deer's blood that my heart means no ill.   35

Boyet. Do not curst° wives hold that self-sovereignty
Only for praise sake, when they strive to be
Lords o'er their lords?

Princess. Only for praise, and praise we may afford
To any lady that subdues a lord.   40

                Enter [Costard, the] Clown.

Boyet. Here comes a member of the commonwealth.°

---

16 **paint** flatter   17 **mend the brow** make the brow more beautiful
18 **good my glass** my fine mirror   21 **saved by merit** saved by what
I truly deserve   22 **heresy in fair** heresy with respect to beauty
24 **mercy goes to kill** (the merciful huntsman goes forth to kill—
instead of leaving the prey wounded—but such killing is not well
regarded)   31 **Glory** i.e., ambition for glory   36 **curst** peevish
41 **member of the commonwealth** i.e., one of our group

Costard. God dig-you-den° all! Pray you, which is
the head lady?

Princess. Thou shalt know her, fellow, by the rest
45   that have no heads.

Costard. Which is the greatest lady, the highest?

Princess. The thickest and the tallest.

Costard. The thickest and the tallest—it is so. Truth
is truth.
   And° your waist, mistress, were as slender as my
50   wit,
   One o' these maids' girdles for your waist should
   be fit.
   Are not you the chief woman? You are the thickest
   here.

Princess. What's your will, sir? What's your will?

Costard. I have a letter from Monsieur Berowne to
one Lady Rosaline.

Princess. O thy letter, thy letter! He's a good friend
55   of mine.
   Stand aside, good bearer. Boyet, you can carve°—
   Break up this capon.°

Boyet.   I am bound to serve.
   This letter is mistook; it importeth° none here.
   It is writ to Jaquenetta.

Princess.   We will read it, I swear.
   Break the neck° of the wax, and every one give
60   ear.

Boyet. (*Reads*) "By heaven, that thou art fair is
most infallible; true that thou art beauteous; truth
itself that thou art lovely. More fairer than fair,
beautiful than beauteous, truer than truth itself,

---

42 **God dig-you-den** God give you good evening 50 **And if** 56
carve (with pun on the sense "flirt") 57 **Break up this capon** (1)
carve this chicken (2) open this love-letter 58 **importeth** concerns
60 **Break the neck** (still referring to the capon)

have commiseration on thy heroical vassal. The 65
magnanimous and most illustrate° king Cophetua
set eye upon the pernicious and indubitate° beggar
Zenelophon,° and he it was that might rightly say
veni, vidi, vici; which to annothanize° in the vulgar
(O base and obscure vulgar!) *videlicet,°* he came, 70
saw, and overcame. He came, one; saw, two;
overcame, three. Who came? The king. Why did
he come? To see. Why did he see? To overcome.
To whom came he? To the beggar. What saw he?
The beggar. Who overcame he? The beggar. The 75
conclusion is victory. On whose side? The king's.
The captive is enriched. On whose side? The beggar's. The catastrophe is a nuptial. On whose side?
The king's. No—on both in one, or one in both.
I am the king, for so stands the comparison, thou 80
the beggar, for so witnesseth thy lowliness. Shall
I command thy love? I may. Shall I enforce thy
love? I could. Shall I entreat thy love? I will. What
shalt thou exchange for rags? Robes. For tittles?°
Titles. For thyself? Me. Thus, expecting thy reply, 85
I profane my lips on thy foot, my eyes on thy pic-
ture, and my heart on thy every part.
    Thine in the dearest design of industry,°
                    Don Adriano de Armado.
Thus dost thou hear the Nemean lion° roar 90
    'Gainst thee, thou lamb, that standest as his prey.
Submissive fall his princely feet before,
    And he from forage° will incline to play.
But if thou strive, poor soul, what art thou then?
Food for his rage, repasture° for his den." 95

Princess. What plume of feathers is he that indited°
    this letter?

66 **illustrate** illustrious   67 **indubitate** undoubted   68 **Zenelophon**
(character in the ballad of King Cophetua and the Beggar)   69 **an-
nothanize** anatomize (or a mock-Latin word to mean "annotate")
70 **videlicet** namely (Latin)   84 **tittles** small jottings in ink   88 **in-
dustry** faithful service   90 **Nemean lion** (lion killed by Hercules)
93 **from forage** turning away from feeding   95 **repasture** food
96 **indited** wrote

What vane?° What weathercock?° Did you ever
hear better?

Boyet. I am much deceived but I remember the style.

Princess. Else your memory is bad, going o'er it ere-
while.

Boyet. This Armado is a Spaniard that keeps here in
100   court;
A phantasime,° a Monarcho,° and one that makes
sport
To the prince and his book-mates.

Princess.   Thou fellow, a word.
Who gave thee this letter?

Costard.   I told you—my lord.

Princess. To whom shouldst thou give it?

Costard.   From my lord to my lady.

105 *Princess.* From which lord to which lady?

Costard. From my lord Berowne, a good master of
mine,
To a lady of France that he called Rosaline.

Princess. Thou hast mistaken° his letter. Come, lords,
away.
Here, sweet, put up this; 'twill be thine another day.
        [*Exeunt Princess and Train. Boyet remains.*]

Boyet. Who is the suitor?° Who is the suitor?

110 *Rosaline.*   Shall I teach you to know?

Boyet. Ay, my continent° of beauty.

Rosaline.   Why, she that bears the bow.
Finely put off!°

---

97 **vane** weather-vane   97 **weather-cock** ostentatious thing   101
phantasime person of wild imaginings   101 **Monarcho** (nickname of
a crazy Italian at the court of Elizabeth)   108 **mistaken** taken to
the wrong person   110 **suitor** (pronounced "shooter")   111 **continent** container   112 **put off** repulsed

Boyet. My lady goes to kill horns, but, if thou marry,
Hang me by the neck if horns that year miscarry.°
Finely put on!°   *115*

Rosaline. Well then, I am the shooter.

Boyet.   And who is your deer?

Rosaline. If we choose by the horns, yourself. Come
not near.
Finely put on indeed!

Maria. You still wrangle with her, Boyet, and she
strikes at the brow.°

Boyet. But she herself is hit lower. Have I hit her
now?   *120*

Rosaline. Shall I come upon thee with an old saying
that was a man when King Pepin of France was a
little boy, as touching the hit it?°

Boyet. So I may answer thee with one as old, that was
a woman when Queen Guinever of Britain was a   *125*
little wench, as touching the hit it.

Rosaline. "Thou canst not hit it, hit it, hit it,
Thou canst not hit it, my good man.

Boyet.   "And° I cannot, cannot, cannot,
And I cannot, another can."   *130*
                    Exit [*Rosaline with Katharine*].

Costard. By my troth, most pleasant, how both did
fit it!

Maria. A mark marvelous well shot, for they both did
hit it.

Boyet. A mark! O, mark but that mark!° A mark,
says my lady!

---

114 **if horns that year miscarry** i.e., if someone is not made a
cuckold   115 **put on** lay on, as a blow   119 **strikes at the brow**
takes careful aim (with an allusion to the cuckold's horns)   123 **hit
it** name of a dance tune (leading to pun on the sense of *hit* = to
copulate)   129 **And** if   133 **mark** (1) target (2) pudend

Let the mark have a prick° in 't, to mete° at if it
may be.

Maria. Wide o' the bow hand!° I' faith, your hand
135   is out.

Costard. Indeed 'a must shoot nearer, or he'll ne'er
hit the clout.°

Boyet. And if my hand be out, then belike your hand
is in.

Costard. Then will she get the upshoot° by cleaving
the pin.°

Maria. Come, come, you talk greasily;° your lips grow
foul.

Costard. She's too hard for you at pricks, sir. Chal-
140   lenge her to bowl.

Boyet. I fear too much rubbing.° Good night, my
good owl.

> [*Exeunt Boyet and Maria.*]

Costard. By my soul, a swain,° a most simple clown!
Lord, lord, how the ladies and I have put him
down!
O' my troth,° most sweet jests, most incony° vul-
gar wit.
When it comes so smoothly off, so obscenely as it
145   were, so fit!
Armado to th' one side—O, a most dainty man!
To see him walk before a lady, and to bear her fan!
To see him kiss his hand, and how most sweetly
'a will swear!

---

134 **prick** mark within the target (with additional bawdy suggestion)
134 **mete** aim   135 **Wide o' the bow hand** far from the target on
the bow-hand side   136 **clout** nail in the center of the target
138 **upshoot** best shot   138 **cleaving the pin** (1) striking the center
of the target (2) causing emission in the male   139 **greasily** in-
decently   141 **rubbing** (bowling balls striking each other; with
sexual innuendo)   142 **swain** herdsman   144 **O' my troth** by my
faith   144 **incony** fine

And his page o' t' other side, that handful of wit,
Ah, heavens, it is a most pathetical nit!°   *150*
                                        Shout within.
Sola,° sola!   [*Exit.*]

[Scene II. *The park.*]

Enter Dull, Holofernes the Pedant, and Nathaniel.

Nathaniel. Very reverend sport, truly, and done in
the testimony° of a good conscience.

Holofernes. The deer was, as you know, *sanguis,* in
blood; ripe as the pomewater,° who now hangeth
like a jewel in the ear of *coelo,* the sky, the welkin,   *5*
the heaven; and anon falleth like a crab° on the
face of *terra,* the soil, the land, the earth.

Nathaniel. Truly, Master Holofernes, the epithets are
sweetly varied, like a scholar at the least. But sir,
I assure ye it was a buck of the first head.°   *10*

Holofernes. Sir Nathaniel, *haud credo.*°

Dull. 'Twas not a *haud credo,* 'twas a pricket.°

Holofernes. Most barbarous intimation!° Yet a kind
of insinuation, as it were, *in via,* in way, of expli-
cation;° *facere,*° as it were, replication,° or rather,   *15*
ostentare, to show, as it were, his inclination—after
his undressed, unpolished, uneducated, unpruned,
untrained, or, rather, unlettered, or, ratherest, un-

---

150 **nit** small thing (louse) 151 **Sola** (a hunting cry) IV.ii.2 **testi-
mony** approval 4 **pomewater** (variety of a sweet apple) 6 **crab**
crab apple 10 **buck of the first head** full-grown buck 11 **haud
credo** I do not believe it (Latin; in the next line, Dull apparently
takes the words as *old gray doe*) 12 **pricket** two-year old red deer
13 **intimation** (a pedantic substitute for "insinuation") 14–15 **ex-
plication** explanation 15 **facere** to make 15 **replication** unfold-
ing, revelation

confirmed fashion—to insert again my *haud credo*
20 for a deer.

Dull. I said the deer was not a *haud credo,* 'twas a
pricket.

Holofernes. Twice sod° simplicity, *bis coctus!*°
O thou monster Ignorance, how deformed dost
thou look!

Nathaniel. Sir, he hath never fed of the dainties that
25   are bred in a book.
He hath not eat paper, as it were, he hath not
drunk ink. His intellect is not replenished. He is
only an animal, only sensible in the duller parts.
And such barren plants are set before us that we
thankful should be,
Which we of taste and feeling are, for those parts
30   that do fructify° in us more than he.
For as it would ill become me to be vain, indiscreet, or a fool,
So were there a patch° set on learning, to see him
in a school.
But, *omne bene,*° say I, being of an old father's
mind,
Many can brook° the weather that love not the
wind.

Dull. You two are book-men. Can you tell me by
35   your wit
What was a month old at Cain's birth that's not
five weeks old as yet?

Holofernes. Dictynna,° goodman Dull. Dictynna,
goodman Dull.

Dull. What is Dictynna?

Nathaniel. A title to Phoebe, to Luna, to the moon.

---

23 **Twice sod** soaked twice (again and again)   23 **bis coctus** cooked
twice   30 **fructify** bear fruit   32 **patch** fool   33 **omne bene** all is
well   34 **brook** endure   37 **Dictynna** Diana, the moon

Holofernes. The moon was a month old when Adam
    was no more,   40
  And raught° not to five weeks when he came to
    fivescore.
  Th' allusion holds in the exchange.°

Dull. 'Tis true indeed; the collusion° holds in the ex-
    change.

Holofernes. God comfort thy capacity! I say th' allu-   45
  sion holds in the exchange.

Dull. And I say the pollution holds in the exchange,
  for the moon is never but a month old; and I say
  beside that 'twas a pricket that the princess killed.

Holofernes. Sir Nathaniel, will you hear an extempo- 50
  ral° epitaph on the death of the deer? And, to
  humor the ignorant, I call the deer the princess
  killed, a pricket.

Nathaniel. Perge,° good Master Holofernes, *perge,* so
  it shall please you to abrogate scurrility.°   55

Holofernes. I will something affect the letter° for it
  argues facility.
  The preyful° princess pierced and pricked a pretty
    pleasing pricket;
  Some say a sore,° but not a sore till now made sore
    with shooting.
  The dogs did yell. Put L° to sore, then sorel° jumps
    from thicket;
  Or pricket, sore, or else sorel. The people fall a
    hooting.   60
  If sore be sore, then L to sore makes fifty sores—
    o' sorel.

---

41 **raught** attained   42 **Th' allusion . . . exchange** (the riddle serves
for Adam as well as for Cain)   43 **collusion** (a pedantic misunder-
standing)   50–51 **extemporal** on the spur of the moment   54 **Perge**
continue   55 **abrogate scurrility** put aside foul talk   56 **affect the
letter** alliterate   57 **preyful** killing much prey   58 **sore** four-year
old buck   59 **L** (the Roman numeral fifty)   59 **sorel** young buck

Of one sore I an hundred make by adding but one
more L.

Nathaniel. A rare talent!°

Dull. If a talent be a claw, look how he claws° him
65 with a talent.

Holofernes. This is a gift that I have, simple, simple;
a foolish extravagant spirit, full of forms, figures,
shapes, objects, ideas, apprehensions, motions, rev-
olutions. These are begot in the ventricle° of mem-
70 ory, nourished in the womb of *pia mater,*° and delivered upon the mellowing of occasion.° But the
gift is good in those in whom it is acute, and I am
thankful for it.

Nathaniel. Sir, I praise the Lord for you, and so may
75 my parishioners, for their sons are well tutored by
you, and their daughters profit very greatly under
you. You are a good member of the commonwealth.

Holofernes. Mehercle,° if their sons be ingenious, they
shall want no instruction; if their daughters be ca-
80 pable, I will put it to them. But *vir sapit qui pauca
loquitur.*° A soul feminine saluteth us.

Enter Jaquenetta and [Costard,] the Clown.

Jaquenetta. God give you good morrow, Master Parson.

Holofernes. Master Parson, *quasi*° pierce-one? And if
85 one should be pierced, which is the one?

Costard. Marry, Master Schoolmaster, he that is likest
to a hogshead.°

Holofernes. Of piercing a hogshead!° A good luster

---

63 **talent** talon   64 **claws** flatters   69 **ventricle** part of the brain
containing the memory   70 **pia mater** membrane enclosing the
brain   71 **mellowing of occasion** fit time   78 **Mehercle** By Hercules
80–81 **vir . . . loquitur** "the man is wise who speaks little"   84 **quasi**
as if   87 **hogshead** fathead   88 **piercing a hogshead** getting drunk

of conceit° in a turf° of earth, fire enough for a
flint, pearl enough for a swine. 'Tis pretty; it is well.   *90*

Jaquenetta. Good Master Parson, be so good as read
me this letter. It was given me by Costard, and
sent me from Don Armado. I beseech you read it.

*Holofernes. Fauste, precor, gelida quando pecus omne
sub umbra ruminat,*° and so forth. Ah, good old   *95*
Mantuan. I may speak of thee as the traveler doth
of Venice:

> *Venetia, Venetia,*
> *Chi non ti vede, non ti pretia.*°

Old Mantuan, old Mantuan! Who understandeth   *100*
thee not, loves thee not. *Ut, re, sol, la, mi, fa.* Under pardon, sir, what are the contents? Or, rather,
as Horace says in his—What, my soul, verses?

Nathaniel. Ay, sir, and very learned.

Holofernes. Let me hear a staff,° a stanze, a verse.   *105*
Lege, domine.°

[*Nathaniel reads.*] "If love make me forsworn, how
    shall I swear to love?
   Ah, never faith could hold if not to beauty
    vowed!
Though to myself forsworn, to thee I'll faithful
    prove;
   Those thoughts to me were oaks, to thee like
    osiers bowed.   *110*
Study his bias leaves° and makes his book thine
    eyes,
   Where all those pleasures live that art would
    comprehend.
If knowledge be the mark, to know thee shall suf-
    fice:

88–89 **luster of conceit** brilliant idea   89 **turf** clod   94–95 **Fauste
. . . ruminat** "I pray thee, Faustus, when all the cattle ruminate
beneath the cool shade" (a quotation from a Latin poem by Mantuan, an Italian Renaissance poet)   98–99 **Venetia . . . pretia** "Venice, Venice, only those who do not see thee do not value thee"
(Italian)   105 **staff** stanza   106 **Lege, domine** read, master   111
Study his bias leaves (the student leaves his favorite studies)

Well learnèd is that tongue that well can thee
    commend,
All ignorant that soul that sees thee without won-
115   der;
    Which is to me some praise, that I thy parts
        admire.
Thy eye Jove's lightning bears, thy voice his dread-
    ful thunder,
    Which, not to anger bent, is music and sweet fire.
Celestial as thou art, O pardon love this wrong,
That sings heaven's praise with such an earthly
120   tongue!"

Holofernes. You find not the apostrophus,° and so
    miss the accent. Let me supervise the canzonet.°
    Here are only numbers ratified;° but, for the ele-
    gancy, facility, and golden cadence of poesy, *caret.*°
125 Ovidius Naso was the man; and why indeed
    "Naso"° but for smelling out the odoriferous flow-
    ers of fancy, the jerks of invention?° *Imitari*° is
    nothing. So doth the hound his master, the ape his
    keeper, the tired horse his rider. But, damosella
130 virgin, was this directed to you?

Jaquenetta. Ay, sir, from one Monsieur Berowne, one
    of the strange° queen's lords.

Holofernes. I will overglance the superscript.° "To
    the snow-white hand of the most beauteous Lady
135 Rosaline." I will look again on the intellect° of the
    letter for the nomination° of the party writing to
    the person written unto. "Your ladyship's, in all
    desired employment, Berowne." Sir Nathaniel, this
    Berowne is one of the votaries° with the king; and
140 here he hath framed° a letter to a sequent° of the

---

121 **apostrophus** (mark of punctuation taking the place of a vowel)
122 **canzonet** song   123 **numbers ratified** rhythm regularized   124
caret it is deficient   126 **Naso** nose   127 **jerks of invention** clever
strokes of wit   127 **Imitari** to imitate   132 **strange** foreign   133
superscript address   135 **intellect** purport   136 **nomination** name
139 **votaries** persons who have taken a vow   140 **framed** devised
140 **sequent** follower

stranger queen's, which accidentally, or by the way
of progression,° hath miscarried. Trip and go,° my
sweet, deliver this paper into the royal hand of the
king; it may concern much. Stay not thy compliment;° I forgive thy duty. Adieu.   *145*

Jaquenetta. Good Costard, go with me. Sir, God save
your life.

Costard. Have with thee, my girl.
                              Exit [with Jaquenetta].

Nathaniel. Sir, you have done this in the fear of God
very religiously; and as a certain father saith—   *150*

Holofernes. Sir, tell not me of the father, I do fear
colorable colors.° But to return to the verses—did
they please you, Sir Nathaniel?

Nathaniel. Marvelous well for the pen.°

Holofernes. I do dine today at the father's of a certain   *155*
pupil of mine, where, if before repast it shall please
you to gratify the table with a grace, I will, on my
privilege I have with the parents of the foresaid
child or pupil, undertake your *ben venuto;*° where
I will prove those verses to be very unlearned,   *160*
neither savoring of poetry, wit, nor invention. I beseech your society.

Nathaniel. And thank you too, for society (saith the
text) is the happiness of life.

Holofernes. And, certes,° the text most infallibly con-   *165*
cludes it. [*To Dull*] Sir, I do invite you too; you
shall not say me nay. *Pauca verba.*° Away! The
gentles are at their game, and we will to our recreation.   *Exeunt.*

141–42 **by the way of progression** on its way   142 **Trip and go**
(phrase used of a morris dance)   144–45 **Stay not thy compliment**
do not wait on ceremony   152 **colorable colors** plausible excuses
154 **pen** penmanship, or style of writing   159 **ben venuto** welcome
(Italian)   165 **certes** certainly   167 **Pauca verba** few words

[Scene III. *The park.*]

Enter Berowne with a paper in his hand, alone.

Berowne. The king he is hunting the deer; I am cours-
ing° myself. They have pitched a toil;° I am toiling
in a pitch—pitch that defiles. Defile—a foul word!
Well, set thee down, sorrow, for so they say the
5   fool said, and so say I, and I the fool. Well proved,
wit! By the Lord, this love is as mad as Ajax:°
it kills sheep; it kills me—I a sheep. Well proved
again o' my side! I will not love; if I do, hang me!
I' faith, I will not. O but her eye! By this light, but
10   for her eye, I would not love her—yes, for her two
eyes. Well, I do nothing in the world but lie, and
lie in my throat. By heaven, I do love, and it hath
taught me to rhyme, and to be melancholy; and here
is part of my rhyme, and here my melancholy. Well,
15   she hath one o' my sonnets already. The clown
bore it, the fool sent it, and the lady hath it—
sweet clown, sweeter fool, sweetest lady! By the
world, I would not care a pin if the other three
were in. Here comes one with a paper. God give
20   him grace to groan!   *He stands aside.*

The King ent'reth [with a paper].

King. Ay me!

Berowne. [*Aside*] Shot, by heaven! Proceed, sweet
Cupid. Thou hast thumped him with thy bird-bolt°
under the left pap.° In faith, secrets!

IV.iii.1–2 **coursing** chasing   2 **pitched a toil** set a snare   6 **Ajax**
(ancient Greek warrior who, going mad, killed sheep, believing
them his enemies)   23 **bird-bolt** arrow for shooting birds   24 **pap**
breast

King. [*Reads*] "So sweet a kiss the golden sun gives
    not   25
    To those fresh morning drops upon the rose,
As thy eye-beams when their fresh rays have smote
    The night of dew that on my cheeks down flows.
Nor shines the silver moon one half so bright
    Through the transparent bosom of the deep   30
As doth thy face, through tears of mine, give light.
    Thou shin'st in every tear that I do weep;
No drop but as a coach doth carry thee.
    So ridest thou triumphing in my woe.
Do but behold the tears that swell in me,   35
    And they thy glory through my grief will show.
But do not love thyself—then thou will keep
My tears for glasses° and still make me weep.
O queen of queens, how far dost thou excel
No thought can think, nor tongue of mortal tell!"   40
How shall she know my griefs? I'll drop the paper.
Sweet leaves, shade folly. Who is he comes here?

Enter Longaville [*with a paper*]. *The King steps aside.*

What, Longaville, and reading! Listen, ear.

Berowne. Now, in thy likeness, one more fool appear!

Longaville. Ay me, I am forsworn.   45

Berowne. Why, he comes in like a perjure,° wearing
    papers.°

King. In love, I hope—sweet fellowship in shame!

Berowne. One drunkard loves another of the name.

Longaville. Am I the first that have been perjured so?   50

Berowne. I could put thee in comfort—not by two
    that I know.

---

38 **glasses** mirrors 46 **perjure** perjurer 46 **wearing papers** (a punishment for perjury, to wear a paper on the head as a public shame; presumably Longaville has a sonnet in his hatband)

Thou makest the triumviry,° the corner-cap° of
    society,
The shape of Love's Tyburn,° that hangs up sim-
    plicity.

Longaville. I fear these stubborn lines lack power to
    move.
55 O sweet Maria, empress of my love!
These numbers will I tear, and write in prose.

Berowne. O, rhymes are guards° on wanton Cupid's
    hose;
Disfigure not his shop.°

Longaville.   This same shall go.

He reads the sonnet.

"Did not the heavenly rhetoric of thine eye,
60   'Gainst whom the world cannot hold argument,
Persuade my heart to this false perjury?
    Vows for thee broke deserve not punishment.
A woman I forswore, but I will prove,
    Thou being a goddess, I forswore not thee.
65 My vow was earthly, thou a heavenly love;
    Thy grace, being gained, cures all disgrace in me.
Vows are but breath, and breath a vapor is;
    Then thou, fair sun, which on my earth dost
        shine,
Exhal'st this vapor-vow; in thee it is.
70   If broken then, it is no fault of mine;
If by me broke, what fool is not so wise
To lose an oath to win a paradise?"

Berowne. This is the liver-vein,° which makes flesh a
    deity,
A green goose° a goddess. Pure, pure idolatry.

52 **triumviry** triumvirate   52 **corner-cap** cap with corners (worn
by divines, judges, and scholars) 53 **Tyburn** place of execution
(the triangular-shaped gallows bears a resemblance to a corner-cap)
57 **guards** ornaments 58 **shop** organ of generation, or codpiece
73 **liver-vein** vein coming from the liver (the place of the origin of
love) 74 **green goose** goose born the previous autumn (and so, a
young girl)

God amend us, God amend! We are much out o'
th' way.°   75

Enter Dumaine [with a paper].

Longaville. By whom shall I send this?—Company?
Stay.   [*Steps aside.*]

Berowne. All hid,° all hid—an old infant play.
Like a demi-god here sit I in the sky,
And wretched fools' secrets heedfully o'er-eye.
More sacks to the mill°—O heavens, I have my
wish!   80
Dumaine transformed! Four woodcocks° in a dish!

Dumaine. O most divine Kate!

Berowne. O most profane coxcomb!

Dumaine. By heaven, the wonder in a mortal eye!

Berowne. By earth, she is not, Corporal.° There you
lie!   85

Dumaine. Her amber hairs for foul hath amber
quoted.°

Berowne. An amber-colored raven was well noted.

Dumaine. As upright as the cedar.

Berowne.   Stoop,° I say—
Her shoulder is with child.°

Dumaine.   As fair as day.

Berowne. Ay, as some days; but then no sun must
shine.   90

Dumaine. O that I had my wish!

75 **out o' th' way** on the wrong track   77 **All hid** (formula from a
child's game)   80 **More sacks to the mill** more yet to do   81 **wood-
cocks** silly birds   85 **Corporal** officer (with a pun on the word for
bodily, human)   86 **Her amber . . . quoted** her amber-colored hair
made amber look ugly by contrast   88 **Stoop** stooped   89 **with
child** i.e., rounded

Longaville.   And I had mine!

King. And I mine too, good Lord!

Berowne. Amen, so I had mine! Is not that a good
    word?

Dumaine. I would forget her, but a fever she
95   Reigns in my blood, and will rememb'red be.

Berowne. A fever in your blood? Why, then incision
    Would let her out in saucers. Sweet misprision!°

Dumaine. Once more I'll read the ode that I have writ.

Berowne. Once more I'll mark how love can vary wit.

Dumaine reads his sonnet.

100 *Dumaine.* "On a day—alack the day!—
          Love, whose month is ever May,
          Spied a blossom passing fair
          Playing in the wanton air.
          Through the velvet leaves the wind,
105   All unseen, can passage find;
          That the lover, sick to death,
          Wished himself the heaven's breath.
          Air, quoth he, thy cheeks may blow;
          Air, would I might triumph so!
110   But, alack, my hand is sworn
          Ne'er to pluck thee from thy thorn.
          Vow, alack, for youth unmeet,
          Youth so apt to pluck a sweet!
          Do not call it sin in me,
115   That I am forsworn for thee;
          Thou for whom Jove would swear
          Juno but an Ethiop° were,
          And deny himself for Jove,
          Turning mortal for thy love."
120   This will I send, and something else more plain,
      That shall express my true love's fasting pain.°

97 **misprision** mistake   117 **Ethiop** black person   121 **fasting pain**
pain caused by deprivation

O, would the king, Berowne, and Longaville
Were lovers too! Ill, to example ill,
Would from my forehead wipe a perjured note,°
For none offend where all alike do dote.   125

Longaville. [*Advancing*] Dumaine, thy love is far from
    charity,
That in love's grief desir'st society.
You may look pale, but I should blush, I know,
To be o'erheard and taken napping so.

King. [*Advancing*] Come, sir, you blush! As his your
    case is such;   130
You chide at him, offending twice as much.
You do not love Maria! Longaville
Did never sonnet for her sake compile,
Nor never lay his wreathèd arms athwart
His loving bosom to keep down his heart.   135
I have been closely shrouded in this bush,
And marked you both, and for you both did blush.
I heard your guilty rhymes, observed your fashion,
Saw sighs reek° from you, noted well your passion.
"Ay me!" says one; "O Jove!" the other cries.   140
One, her hairs were gold; crystal, the other's eyes.
[*To Longaville*] You would for paradise break faith
    and troth,
[*To Dumaine*] And Jove, for your love, would in-
    fringe an oath.
What will Berowne say when that he shall hear
Faith infringèd, which such zeal did swear?   145
How will he scorn, how will he spend his wit!
How will he triumph, leap and laugh at it!
For all the wealth that ever I did see,
I would not have him know so much by me.°

Berowne. [*Advancing*] Now step I forth to whip hy-
    pocrisy.   150
Ah, good my liege, I pray thee pardon me.
Good heart, what grace hast thou, thus to reprove

123–24 **Ill . . . note** wickedness, not liking to make itself an example,
would remove from me the papers I bear as the punishment **for**
perjury   139 **reek** exhale   149 **by me** concerning me

These worms for loving, that art most in love?
Your eyes do make no coaches;° in your tears
155 There is no certain princess that appears.
You'll not be perjured, 'tis a hateful thing.
Tush, none but minstrels like of sonneting!
But are you not ashamed? Nay, are you not,
All three of you, to be thus much o'ershot?°
160 You found his mote, the king your mote did see;
But I a beam° do find in each of three.
O what a scene of fool'ry have I seen,
Of sighs, of groans, of sorrow, and of teen!°
O me, with what strict patience have I sat,
165 To see a king transformèd to a gnat!
To see great Hercules whipping a gig,°
And profound Solomon to tune a jig,
And Nestor° play at push-pin° with the boys,
And critic Timon° laugh at idle toys!
170 Where lies thy grief? O, tell me, good Dumaine.
And, gentle Longaville, where lies thy pain?
And where my liege's? All about the breast.
A caudle,° ho!

King.   Too bitter is thy jest.
Are we betrayed thus to thy over-view?

175 Berowne. Not you by me, but I betrayed to you;
I that am honest, I that hold it sin
To break the vow I am engagèd in,
I am betrayed by keeping company
With men like you, men of inconstancy.
180 When shall you see me write a thing in rhyme?
Or groan for Joan? Or spend a minute's time
In pruning° me? When shall you hear that I
Will praise a hand, a foot, a face, an eye,
A gait, a state, a brow, a breast, a waist,
A leg, a limb—

154 coaches (for love to ride in—as in line 33)   159 o'ershot wide
of the mark   160–61 mote . . . beam (the contrast is between small
and large faults; see Matthew 7:3-5; Luke 6:41-42)   163 teen grief
166 gig top   168 Nestor ancient Greek sage   168 push-pin child's
game   169 critic Timon Greek misanthrope   173 caudle healing
drink for an invalid   182 pruning preening

King.   Soft!° Whither away so fast?   *185*
   A true° man or a thief, that gallops so?

Berowne. I post° from love. Good lover, let me go.

    Enter Jaquenetta and [Costard, the] Clown.

Jaquenetta. God bless the king!

King.   What present hast thou there?

Costard. Some certain treason.

King.   What makes° treason here?

Costard. Nay, it makes nothing, sir.

King.   If it mar nothing neither,   *190*
   The treason and you go in peace away together.

Jaquenetta. I beseech your Grace let this letter be read.
   Our parson misdoubts° it; 'twas treason, he said.

King. Berowne, read it over.
            He [Berowne] reads the letter.
   Where hadst thou it?

Jaquenetta. Of Costard.

King. Where hadst thou it?   *195*

Costard. Of Dun Adramadio, Dun Adramadio.
            [Berowne tears the letter.]

King. How now, what is in you? Why dost thou tear it?

Berowne. A toy, my liege, a toy. Your Grace needs
   not fear it.   *200*

Longaville. It did move him to passion, and therefore
   let's hear it.

Dumaine. [*Gathering up the pieces*] It is Berowne's
   writing, and here is his name.

---

185 **Soft** wait a minute (an exclamation)   186 **true** honest   187 **post**
ride in haste   189 **makes** does   193 **misdoubts** mistrusts

Berowne. [*To Costard*] Ah, you whoreson loggerhead,° you were born to do me shame!
Guilty, my lord, guilty. I confess, I confess.

205 *King*. What?

Berowne. That you three fools lacked me fool to make
up the mess.°
He, he, and you—and you, my liege, and I,
Are pick-purses in love, and we deserve to die.
O dismiss this audience, and I shall tell you more.

Dumaine. Now the number is even.

210 *Berowne*.   True, true, we are four.
Will these turtles° be gone?

King.   Hence, sirs, away!

Costard. Walk aside the true folk, and let the traitors
stay.   [*Exeunt Costard and Jaquenetta*.]

Berowne. Sweet lords, sweet lovers, O let us embrace!
As true we are as flesh and blood can be.
215 The sea will ebb and flow, heaven show his face;
Young blood doth not obey an old decree.
We cannot cross° the cause why we were born;
Therefore of all hands must we be forsworn.

King. What, did these rent° lines show some love of
thine?

Berowne. Did they? quoth you. Who sees the heavenly
220   Rosaline,
That, like a rude and savage man of Inde
At the first op'ning of the gorgeous East,
Bows not his vassal head and, strooken blind,
Kisses the base ground with obedient breast?
225 What peremptory° eagle-sighted eye
Dares look upon the heaven of her brow
That is not blinded by her majesty?

---

203 **whoreson loggerhead** rascally blockhead   206 **mess** party of
four at table   211 **turtles** turtledoves, lovers   217 **cross** thwart
219 **rent** damaged   225 **peremptory** resolute

King. What zeal, what fury, hath inspired thee now?
My love, her mistress, is a gracious moon;
She, an attending star, scarce seen a light.   230

Berowne. My eyes are then no eyes, nor I Berowne.
O, but for my love, day would turn to night!
Of all complexions the culled sovereignty°
Do meet, as at a fair, in her fair cheek,
Where several worthies° make one dignity,   235
Where nothing wants° that want itself doth seek.
Lend me the flourish° of all gentle tongues—
Fie, painted rhetoric!° O, she needs it not!
To things of sale° a seller's praise belongs:
She passes praise; then praise too short doth blot.   240
A withered hermit, five-score winters worn,
Might shake off fifty, looking in her eye.
Beauty doth varnish° age as if new-born,
And gives the crutch the cradle's infancy.
O, 'tis the sun that maketh all things shine.   245

King. By heaven, thy love is black as ebony!

Berowne. Is ebony like her? O wood divine!
A wife of such wood were felicity.
O, who can give an oath? Where is a book?
That I may swear beauty doth beauty lack   250
If that she learn not of her eye to look.
No face is fair that is not full so black.

King. O paradox! Black is the badge of hell,
The hue of dungeons, and the school of night;°
And beauty's crest becomes the heavens well.°   255

Berowne. Devils soonest tempt, resembling spirits of
    light.

---

233 **culled sovereignty** chosen as the best   235 **worthies** good qualities   236 **wants** lacks   237 **flourish** adornment   238 **painted rhetoric** extravagant speech   239 **of sale** for sale   243 **varnish** lend
freshness   254 **school of night** (some editors emend "school" to
"suit" or to "shade," but perhaps the term means a place for learning dark things)   255 **beauty's . . . well** true beauty, which is bright,
is heavenly, but if blackness is taken as the sign of beauty, it would
be ironic to link beauty with heaven, which is the source of light

O, if in black my lady's brows be decked,
It mourns that painting and usurping° hair
Should ravish doters with a false aspect;°
260 And therefore is she born to make black fair.
Her favor° turns the fashion of the days,
For native blood° is counted painting now;
And therefore red that would avoid dispraise
Paints itself black to imitate her brow.

Dumaine. To look like her are chimney-sweepers
265 black.

Longaville. And since her time are colliers° counted
bright.

King. And Ethiops of their sweet complexion crack.°

Dumaine. Dark needs no candles now, for dark is
light.

Berowne. Your mistresses dare never come in rain,
270 For fear their colors should be washed away.

King. 'Twere good yours did; for, sir, to tell you plain,
I'll find a fairer face not washed today.

Berowne. I'll prove her fair or talk till doomsday here.

King. No devil will fright thee then so much as she.

275 *Dumaine.* I never knew man hold vile stuff so dear.

Longaville. Look, here's thy love; [*showing his shoe*]
my foot° and her face see.

Berowne. O, if the streets were pavèd with thine eyes,
Her feet were much too dainty for such tread.

Dumaine. O vile! Then, as she goes, what upward lies
280 The street should see as she walked overhead.

King. But what of this? Are we not all in love?

---

258 **usurping** false   259 **aspect** appearance   261 **favor** complexion
262 **native blood** naturally red complexion   266 **colliers** coal-men
267 **crack** boast   276 **my foot** (he is wearing black shoes)

Berowne. O, nothing so sure, and thereby all forsworn.

King. Then leave this chat, and, good Berowne, now
  prove
Our loving lawful and our faith not torn.

Dumaine. Ay marry, there, some flattery for this evil!   *285*

Longaville. O, some authority how to proceed!
Some tricks, some quillets,° how to cheat the devil!

Dumaine. Some salve for perjury.

Berowne.   O, 'tis more than need!
Have at you, then, affection's men-at-arms!°
Consider what you first did swear unto.   *290*
To fast, to study, and to see no woman—
Flat treason 'gainst the kingly state of youth.
Say, can you fast? Your stomachs are too young,
And abstinence engenders maladies.
[And where that° you have vowed to study, lords,   *295*
In that each of you have forsworn his book,
Can you still dream and pore and thereon look?
For when would you, my lord, or you, or you,
Have found the ground of study's excellence
Without the beauty of a woman's face?   *300*
From women's eyes this doctrine I derive:
They are the ground, the books, the academes,°
From whence doth spring the true Promethean
  fire.°
Why, universal plodding poisons° up
The nimble spirits in the arteries,   *305*
As motion and long-during° action tires
The sinewy vigor of the traveler.
Now for not looking on a woman's face,

---

287 **quillets** subtleties   289 **affection's men-at-arms** love's warriors
295 **where that** whereas (after writing lines 295–316, here bracketed,
Shakespeare apparently decided he could do better, and rewrote the
passage in the ensuing lines, but the printer mistakenly printed
both versions)   302 **academes** academies   303 **Promethean
fire** fire stolen from heaven by Prometheus   304 **poisons** (some editors
emend to *prisons*)   306 **long-during** long-lasting

You have in that forsworn the use of eyes,
310 And study too, the causer of your vow;
For where is any author in the world
Teaches such beauty as a woman's eye?
Learning is but an adjunct to ourself,
And where we are our learning likewise is.
315 Then when ourselves we see in ladies' eyes,
Do we not likewise see our learning there?]
O, we have made a vow to study, lords,
And in that vow we have forsworn our books;
For when would you, my liege, or you, or you,
320 In leaden contemplation have found out
Such fiery numbers° as the prompting eyes
Of beauty's tutors have enriched you with?
Other slow arts entirely keep the brain,
And therefore, finding barren practisers,
325 Scarce show a harvest of their heavy toil;
But love, first learnèd in a lady's eyes,
Lives not alone immurèd in the brain,
But with the motion of all elements,°
Courses as swift as thought in every power,
330 And gives to every power a double power
Above their functions and their offices.
It adds a precious seeing to the eye:
A lover's eyes will gaze an eagle blind.
A lover's ear will hear the lowest sound,
335 When the suspicious head of theft° is stopped.
Love's feeling is more soft and sensible
Than are the tender horns of cockled° snails.
Love's tongue proves dainty Bacchus gross in taste.
For valor, is not Love a Hercules,
340 Still climbing trees in the Hesperides?°
Subtle as Sphinx; as sweet and musical
As bright Apollo's lute, strung with his hair.
And when Love speaks, the voice of all the gods

---

321 **fiery numbers** passionate verses   328 **with the motion of all elements** i.e., with the force of all the components of the universe
335 **the suspicious head of theft** i.e., a thief's hearing, suspicious of every sound   337 **cockled** in shells   340 **Hesperides** (garden where Hercules picked the golden apples)

Make heaven drowsy with the harmony.
Never durst poet touch a pen to write   345
Until his ink were temp'red with Love's sighs.
O, then his lines would ravish savage ears
And plant in tyrants mild humility.
From women's eyes this doctrine I derive.
They sparkle still the right Promethean fire;   350
They are the books, the arts, the academes,
That show, contain, and nourish all the world;
Else none at all in aught proves excellent.
Then fools you were these women to forswear,
Or, keeping what is sworn, you will prove fools.   355
For wisdom's sake, a word that all men love,
Or for love's sake, a word that loves all men,
Or for men's sake, the authors of these women,
Or women's sake, by whom we men are men—
Let us once lose our oaths to find ourselves,   360
Or else we lose ourselves to keep our oaths.
It is religion to be thus forsworn,
For charity itself fulfils the law,°
And who can sever love from charity?

King. Saint Cupid then! And, soldiers, to the field! 365

Berowne. Advance your standards, and upon them,
    lords!
Pell-mell, down with them! But be first advised,
In conflict that you get the sun of them.°

Longaville. Now to plain-dealing. Lay these glozes°
    by.
Shall we resolve to woo these girls of France?   370

King. And win them too! Therefore let us devise
Some entertainment for them in their tents.

Berowne. First from the park let us conduct them
    thither;
Then homeward every man attach the hand

---

363 **charity . . . law** (Romans 13:8: "he that loveth another hath fulfilled the law")   368 **get the sun of them** approach when the sun
is in their eyes   369 **glozes** trivial comments

375   Of his fair mistress. In the afternoon
We will with some strange pastime solace them,
Such as the shortness of the time can shape;
For revels, dances, masks, and merry hours
Forerun fair Love, strewing her way with flowers.

380 *King.* Away, away! No time shall be omitted
That will be time,° and may by us be fitted.

  Berowne. Allons!° *Allons!* Sowed cockle reaped no
corn,°
And justice always whirls in equal measure.
Light wenches may prove plagues to men forsworn;
385 If so, our copper buys no better treasure.   [*Exeunt.*]

---

381 **be time** come to pass   382 **Allons** let's go (French)   382 **Sowed**
. . . corn if weeds are sown, wheat is not reaped

[ACT V

Scene I. *The park.*]

Enter [Holofernes,] the Pedant, [Nathaniel,] the Curate, and Dull, [the Constable].

Holofernes. Satis quid sufficit.°

Nathaniel. I praise God for you, sir. Your reasons° at dinner have been sharp and sententious,° pleasant without scurrility, witty without affection,° audacious without impudency, learned without opinion,° and strange without heresy. I did converse this *quondam*° day with a companion of the king's, who is intituled, nominated, or called, Don Adriano de Armado.

Holofernes. Novi hominem tanquam te.° His humor is lofty, his discourse peremptory,° his tongue filed,° his eye ambitious, his gait majestical, and his general behavior vain, ridiculous, and thrasonical.° He is too picked,° too spruce, too affected, too odd, as it were, too peregrinate,° as I may call it.

V.i.1 **Satis quid sufficit** enough is as good as a feast   2 **reasons** discourses   3 **sententious** full of meaning   4 **affection** affectation 6 **opinion** dogmatism   7 **quondam** former   10 **Novi hominem tanquam te** I know the man as well as I know you   11 **peremptory** decisive   12 **filed** polished   13–14 **thrasonical** boastful   14 **picked** refined   15 **peregrinate** foreign in manner

Nathaniel. A most singular and choice epithet.
                  Draw out his table-book.°

Holofernes. He draweth out the thread of his ver-
bosity finer than the staple° of his argument. I
20   abhor such fanatical phantasimes,° such insociable°
and point-devise° companions; such rackers° of
orthography as to speak "dout" fine when he
should say "doubt," "det" when he should pronounce "debt"—d, e, b, t, not d, e, t. He clepeth°
25   a calf "cauf," half "hauf," neighbor *vocatur*°
"nebor," neigh abbreviated "ne." This is abhomina-
ble, which he would call "abominable." It insinuateth me of insanie.° *Ne intelligis, domine?*° To
make frantic, lunatic.

30   *Nathaniel. Laus Deo bone intelligo.*°

Holofernes. Bone?° *Bone* for *bene!* Priscian° a little
scratched;° 'twill serve.

     Enter [*Armado, the*] *Braggart,* [*Moth, the*] *Boy,*
            [*and Costard, the Clown*].

Nathaniel. Videsne quis venit?°

Holofernes. Video, et gaudeo.°

35   *Armado.* [*To Moth*] *Chirrah!*°

Holofernes. Quare° "chirrah," not "sirrah"?

Armado. Men of peace, well encount'red.

---

17 s.d. **table-book** tablet (stage directions are often, as here, in the
imperative)   19 **staple** fiber   20 **phantasimes** wild imaginers   20
insociable impossible to associate with   21 **point-devise** perfectly
correct   21 **rackers** torturers   24 **clepeth** calls   25 **vocatur** is called
27–28 **insinuateth me of insanie** suggests insanity to me   28 **Ne intelligis, domine** do you not understand, sir?   30 **Laus Deo bone
intelligo** praise be to God, I well understand   31 **Bone** (probably
a mixture of Latin *bene* and French *bon*)   31 **Priscian** Latin gram-
marian of sixth century A.D.   32 **scratched** damaged   33 **Videsne quis
venit?** do you see who is coming?   34 **Video, et gaudeo** I see, and
I rejoice   35 **Chirrah** (dialect form for "sirrah")   36 **Quare** why?

Holofernes. Most military sir, salutation.

Moth. [*Aside to Costard*] They have been at a great
feast of languages and stol'n the scraps.   40

Costard. O, they have lived long on the alms-basket°
of words. I marvel thy master hath not eaten thee
for a word; for thou art not so long by the head
as *honorificabilitudinitatibus.*° Thou art easier swallowed than a flapdragon.°   45

Moth. Peace! The peal° begins.

Armado. Monsieur, are you not lett'red?°

Moth. Yes, yes! He teaches boys the hornbook.°
What is a, b, spelled backward with the horn on
his head?   50

Holofernes. Ba, *pueritia,*° with a horn added.

Moth. Ba, most silly sheep with a horn. You hear his
learning.

Holofernes. Quis,° *quis,* thou consonant?

Moth. The last of the five vowels, if you repeat them;   55
or the fifth, if I.

Holofernes. I will repeat them: a, e, i—

Moth. The sheep. The other two concludes it—o, u.

Armado. Now, by the salt wave of the Mediterranean,
a sweet touch, a quick venew° of wit! Snip, snap,   60
quick and home! It rejoiceth my intellect. True wit!

Moth. Offered by a child to an old man—which is
wit-old.°

---

41 **alms-basket** (basket used at feasts to collect scraps from the table
for the poor)   44 **honorificabilitudinitatibus** (Latin tongue-twister,
thought to be the longest word known)   45 **flapdragon** (burning
raisin or plum floating in liquor, and so drunk)   46 **peal** (of bells)
47 **lett'red** man of letters   48 **hornbook** (parchment with alphabet
and numbers, covered with transparent horn, for teaching spelling
and counting)   51 **pueritia** childishness   54 **Quis** what?   60 **venew**
thrust   63 **wit-old** i.e., mentally feeble (with pun on *wittol* = cuckold)

Holofernes. What is the figure?° What is the figure?

65 *Moth.* Horns.

Holofernes. Thou disputes like an infant. Go whip
thy gig.°

Moth. Lend me your horn to make one, and I will
whip about your infamy *manu cita.*° A gig of a
70 cuckold's horn.

Costard. And° I had but one penny in the world,
thou shouldst have it to buy gingerbread. Hold,
there is the very remuneration I had of thy master,
thou halfpenny purse of wit, thou pigeon-egg of
75 discretion. O, and the heavens were so pleased
that thou wert but my bastard, what a joyful father
wouldest thou make me! Go to, thou hast it *ad
dunghill,*° at the fingers' ends, as they say.

Holofernes. O, I smell false Latin! "Dunghill" for
80 *unguem.*

Armado. Arts-man,° preambulate.° We will be sin-
gled from the barbarous. Do you not educate youth
at the charge-house° on the top of the mountain?

Holofernes. Or *mons,* the hill.

85 *Armado.* At your sweet pleasure, for the mountain.

Holofernes. I do, *sans question.*

Armado. Sir, it is the king's most sweet pleasure and
affection to congratulate the princess at her pavilion
in the posteriors° of this day, which the rude mul-
90 titude call the afternoon.

Holofernes. The posterior of the day, most generous

---

64 **figure** figure of speech   67 **gig** top   69 **manu cita** with a swift
hand   71 **And** if   77–78 **ad dunghill** (perhaps a schoolboy's corrup-
tion of the proverb "ad unguem," to the fingernail, meaning "precisely")   81 **Arts-man** learned man   81 **preambulate** walk forth
83 **charge-house** school (perhaps an allusion to a specific school on
a hill, mentioned by Erasmus)   89 **posteriors** hind parts

sir, is liable, congruent, and measurable° for the
afternoon. The word is well culled, chose, sweet
and apt, I do assure you, sir, I do assure.

Armado. Sir, the king is a noble gentleman, and my　95
familiar,° I do assure ye, very good friend. For
what is inward° between us, let it pass. I do beseech thee, remember thy courtesy.° I beseech thee
apparel thy head. And among other importunate
and most serious designs, and of great import in-　100
deed, too—but let that pass; for I must tell thee,
it will please his Grace, by the world, sometime to
lean upon my poor shoulder, and with his royal
finger thus dally with my excrement,° with my
mustachio—but, sweet heart, let that pass. By the　105
world, I recount no fable! Some certain special
honors it pleaseth his greatness to impart to Armado, a soldier, a man of travel, that hath seen
the world—but let that pass. The very all of all
is (but, sweet heart, I do implore secrecy) that the　110
king would have me present the princess (sweet
chuck) with some delightful ostentation, or show,
or pageant, or antic,° or fire-work. Now, understanding that the curate and your sweet self are
good at such eruptions and sudden breaking out　115
of mirth, as it were, I have acquainted you withal,
to the end to crave your assistance.

Holofernes. Sir, you shall present before her the Nine
Worthies.° Sir Nathaniel, as concerning some entertainment of time, some show in the posterior of　120
this day, to be rend'red by our assistance, the king's
command, and this most gallant, illustrate, and

---

92 **liable, congruent, measurable** (all synonyms for "suitable")　96
familiar close friend　97 **inward** private　98 **remember thy courtesy**
(possibly: remove your hat when the king's name is mentioned)
104 **excrement** that which grows out (such as hair, nails, feathers)
113 **antic** fanciful pageant　118–19 **Nine Worthies** (traditionally,
Hector, Caesar, Joshua, David, Judas Maccabaeus, Alexander, King
Arthur, Charlemagne, Godfrey of Boulogne; here Hercules and
Pompey are included)

learned gentleman, before the princess—I say,
none so fit as to present the Nine Worthies.

125 *Nathaniel.* Where will you find men worthy enough
to present them?

Holofernes. Joshua, yourself; myself; and this gallant
gentleman, Judas Maccabaeus; this swain, because
of his great limb or joint, shall pass° Pompey the
130 Great; the page, Hercules—

Armado. Pardon, sir—error! He is not quantity
enough for that Worthy's thumb; he is not so big
as the end of his club.

Holofernes. Shall I have audience?° He shall present
135 Hercules in minority.° His enter and exit shall be
strangling a snake; and I will have an apology° for
that purpose.

Moth. An excellent device! So if any of the audience
hiss, you may cry, "Well done, Hercules! Now
140 thou crushest the snake!" That is the way to make
an offense gracious, though few have the grace to
do it.

Armado. For the rest of the Worthies?

Holofernes. I will play three myself.

145 *Moth.* Thrice-worthy gentleman!

Armado. Shall I tell you a thing?

Holofernes. We attend.

Armado. We will have, if this fadge° not, an antic.
I beseech you, follow.

150 *Holofernes.* Via,° goodman Dull! Thou hast spoken
no word all this while.

Dull. Nor understood none neither, sir.

---

129 **pass** represent   134 **have audience** be heard   135 **minority** early
youth   136 **apology** justification   148 **fadge** succeed   150 **Via** come
on (Italian)

Holofernes. Allons, we will employ thee.

Dull. I'll make one in a dance, or so; or I will play
    on the tabor° to the Worthies, and let them dance   155
    the hay.°

Holofernes. Most dull, honest Dull! To our sport,
    away!   *Exeunt.*

[Scene II. *The park.*]

*Enter the Ladies [the Princess, Katharine,
Rosaline, and Maria].*

Princess. Sweet hearts, we shall be rich ere we depart
    If fairings° come thus plentifully in.
    A lady walled about with diamonds!
    Look you what I have from the loving king.

Rosaline. Madam, came nothing else along with that?   5

Princess. Nothing but this? Yes, as much love in
    rhyme
    As would be crammed up in a sheet of paper,
    Writ o' both sides the leaf, margent° and all,
    That he was fain° to seal on Cupid's name.

Rosaline. That was the way to make his godhead
    wax,°   10
    For he hath been five thousand year a boy.

Katharine. Ay, and a shrowd° unhappy gallows° too.

Rosaline. You'll ne'er be friends with him: 'a killed
    your sister.

---

155 **tabor** small drum   156 **hay** country dance   V.ii.2 **fairings** presents   8 **margent** margin   9 **fain** eager   10 **wax** grow (and with a
pun on sealing-wax)   12 **shrowd** accursed   12 **gallows** one fit to be
hanged

Katharine. He made her melancholy, sad, and heavy;
15   And so she died. Had she been light, like you,
    Of such a merry, nimble, stirring spirit,
    She might ha' been a grandam ere she died.
    And so may you, for a light heart lives long.

Rosaline. What's your dark meaning, mouse, of this
    light word?

20 *Katharine.* A light condition in a beauty dark.

Rosaline. We need more light to find your meaning
    out.

Katharine. You'll mar the light by taking it in snuff,°
    Therefore, I'll darkly end the argument.

Rosaline. Look what° you do, you do it still i' th'
    dark.

25 *Katharine.* So do not you, for you are a light wench.

Rosaline. Indeed I weigh° not you, and therefore
    light.

Katharine. You weigh me not? O, that's you care not
    for me!

Rosaline. Great reason, for past care is still past cure.

Princess. Well bandied° both! A set of wit well
    played.
30   But Rosaline, you have a favor too—
    Who sent it? And what is it?

Rosaline.   I would you knew.
    And if my face were but as fair as yours,
    My favor were as great. Be witness this.
    Nay, I have verses too, I thank Berowne;
35   The numbers° true, and, were the numb'ring° too,
    I were the fairest goddess on the ground.

---

22 **taking it in snuff** being annoyed   24 **Look what** whatever   26
weigh value at a certain rate   29 **bandied** hit back and forth (figure
from tennis)   35 **numbers** meter   35 **numb'ring** estimate

I am compared to twenty thousand fairs.°
O, he hath drawn my picture in his letter!

Princess. Anything like?

Rosaline. Much in the letters, nothing in the praise. 40

Princess. Beauteous as ink—a good conclusion.

Katharine. Fair as a text B in a copy-book.

Rosaline. 'Ware° pencils, ho! Let me not die your
    debtor,
My red dominical,° my golden letter.
O, that your face were not so full of O's!° 45

Princess. A pox of° that jest, and I beshrow all
    shrows!°
But Katharine, what was sent to you from fair
    Dumaine?

Katharine. Madam, this glove.

Princess.   Did he not send you twain?

Katharine. Yes, madam; and moreover,
Some thousand verses of a faithful lover. 50
A huge translation of hypocrisy,
Vilely compiled, profound simplicity.°

Maria. This, and these pearls, to me sent Longaville.
The letter is too long by half a mile.

Princess. I think no less. Dost thou not wish in heart 55
The chain were longer and the letter short?

Maria. Ay, or I would these hands might never part.

Princess. We are wise girls to mock our lovers so.

Rosaline. They are worse fools to purchase mocking
    so.

---

37 fairs beautiful women   **43 'Ware** beware   **44 red dominical** red
S (for Sunday, the Lord's Day)   45 **O's** smallpox scars   46 **A pox
of** may a plague strike   46 **beshrow all shrows** curse all shrews
52 **simplicity** simple-mindedness

60　　That same Berowne I'll torture ere I go.
　　　O that I knew he were but in by th' week!°
　　　How I would make him fawn, and beg, and seek,
　　　And wait the season, and observe the times,
　　　And spend his prodigal wits in bootless rhymes,
65　　And shape his service wholly to my hests,°
　　　And make him proud to make me proud that jests!
　　　So pertaunt-like° would I o'ersway his state°
　　　That he should be my fool, and I his fate.

　　Princess. None are so surely caught, when they are
　　　　catched,
70　　As wit turned fool. Folly, in wisdom hatched,
　　　Hath wisdom's warrant and the help of school
　　　And wit's own grace to grace a learnèd fool.

　　Rosaline. The blood of youth burns not with such
　　　　excess
　　　As gravity's revolt to wantonness.

75　*Maria.* Folly in fools bears not so strong a note
　　　As fool'ry in the wise when wit doth dote;
　　　Since all the power thereof it doth apply
　　　To prove, by wit, worth in simplicity.

Enter Boyet.

　　Princess. Here comes Boyet, and mirth is in his face.

　　Boyet. O, I am stabbed with laughter! Where's her
80　　　Grace?

　　Princess. Thy news, Boyet?

　　Boyet.　　　　　　　　Prepare, madam, prepare!
　　　Arm, wenches, arm! Encounters mounted are
　　　Against your peace. Love doth approach disguised,
　　　Armèd in arguments; you'll be surprised.
85　　Muster your wits; stand in your own defense,
　　　Or hide your heads like cowards and fly hence.

---

61 **in by th' week** trapped　65 **hests** commands　67 **pertaunt-like**
(like a winning hand [*Pair-taunt*] in a certain card game)　67 **o'ersway his state** overrule his power

Princess. Saint Denis° to Saint Cupid! What are they
　　That charge their breath against us? Say, scout, say.

Boyet. Under the cool shade of a sycamore
　　I thought to close mine eyes some half an hour,　　*90*
　　When, lo, to interrupt my purposed rest,
　　Toward that shade I might behold addrest°
　　The king and his companions! Warily
　　I stole into a neighbor thicket by,
　　And overheard what you shall overhear—　　*95*
　　That, by and by, disguised they will be here.
　　Their herald is a pretty knavish page
　　That well by heart hath conned his embassage.°
　　Action and accent did they teach him there:
　　"Thus must thou speak, and thus thy body bear."　　*100*
　　And ever and anon they made a doubt°
　　Presence majestical would put him out;
　　"For," quoth the king, "an angel shalt thou see,
　　Yet fear not thou, but speak audaciously."
　　The boy replied, "An angel is not evil;　　*105*
　　I should have feared her had she been a devil."
　　With that all laughed and clapped him on the
　　　　shoulder,
　　Making the bold wag by their praises bolder.
　　One rubbed his elbow thus, and fleered,° and swore
　　A better speech was never spoke before.　　*110*
　　Another, with his finger and his thumb,
　　Cried *"Via,* we will do 't, come what will come!"
　　The third he capered and cried, "All goes well!"
　　The fourth turned on the toe,° and down he fell.
　　With that they all did tumble on the ground　　*115*
　　With such a zealous laughter, so profound,
　　That in this spleen° ridiculous appears,
　　To check their folly, passion's solemn tears.

Princess. But what, but what? Come they to visit us?

Boyet. They do, they do, and are apparelled thus—　　*120*

87 **Saint Denis** patron saint of France　92 **addresst** approaching
98 **conned his embassage** learned his commission　101 **made a doubt**
expressed a fear　109 **fleered** grinned　114 **turned on the toe** turned
quickly to leave　117 **spleen** excess of mirth

Like Muscovites or Russians, as I guess.
Their purpose is to parley,° court and dance,
And every one his love-feat° will advance
Unto his several mistress, which they'll know
125 By favors several which they did bestow.

Princess. And will they so? The gallants shall be
    tasked;°
For, ladies, we will every one be masked,
And not a man of them shall have the grace,
Despite of suit,° to see a lady's face.
130 Hold, Rosaline, this favor thou shalt wear,
And then the king will court thee for his dear.
Hold, take thou this, my sweet, and give me thine;
So shall Berowne take me for Rosaline.
And change you favors too; so shall your loves
135 Woo contrary, deceived by these removes.°

Rosaline. Come on, then; wear the favors most in
    sight.°

Katharine. But in this changing what is your intent?

Princess. The effect of my intent is to cross° theirs.
They do it but in mockery merriment,
140 And mock for mock is only my intent.
Their several counsels they unbosom° shall
To loves mistook and so be mocked withal
Upon the next occasion that we meet,
With visages displayed, to talk and greet.

145 *Rosaline.* But shall we dance if they desire us to 't?

Princess. No, to the death° we will not move a foot,
Nor to their penned speech render we no grace,
But while 'tis spoke each turn away her face.

Boyet. Why, that contempt will kill the speaker's
    heart,
150 And quite divorce his memory from his part.

122 **parley** hold a conference   123 **love-feat** exploit prompted by
love   126 **tasked** tested   129 **Despite of suit** in spite of his pleading
135 **removes** changes   136 **most in sight** conspicuously   138 **cross**
thwart   141 **unbosom** confide   146 **to the death** as long as we live

Princess. Therefore I do it, and I make no doubt
    The rest will e'er come in if he be out.
    There's no such sport as sport by sport o'erthrown,
    To make theirs ours, and ours none but our own.
    So shall we stay, mocking intended game,°   *155*
    And they, well mocked, depart away with shame.
                     Sound trumpet.

Boyet. The trumpet sounds. Be masked—the maskers
    come.

                   [The Ladies mask.]

*Enter Blackamoors with music; [Moth,] the Boy,
with a speech, and [the King, Berowne, and] the
rest of the Lords [in Russian dress and] disguised.*

Moth. "All hail, the richest beauties on the earth!"

Boyet. Beauties no richer than rich taffeta.

Moth. "A holy parcel of the fairest dames,   *160*
        The Ladies turn their backs to him.
    That ever turned their backs to mortal views!"

Berowne. "Their eyes," villain, "their eyes!"

Moth. "That ever turned their eyes to mortal views!
    Out—"

Boyet. True. "Out" indeed!   *165*

Moth. "Out of your favors, heavenly spirits, vouch-
    safe
    Not to behold"—

Berowne. "Once to behold," rogue!

Moth. "Once to behold with your sun-beamèd eyes,
    —with your sun-beamèd eyes"—   *170*

Boyet. They will not answer to that epithet.
    You were best call it "daughter-beamèd eyes."

Moth. They do not mark me, and that brings° me out.

155 **game** sport   173 **brings** puts

Berowne. Is this your perfectness? Be gone, you rogue!
[*Exit Moth.*]

Rosaline. What would these strangers? Know their
175   minds, Boyet.
If they do speak our language, 'tis our will
That some plain man recount their purposes.
Know what they would.

Boyet. What would you with the Princess?

180 *Berowne.* Nothing but peace and gentle visitation.

Rosaline. What would they, say they?

Boyet. Nothing but peace and gentle visitation.

Rosaline. Why, that they have, and bid them so be
gone.

Boyet. She says you have it and you may be gone.

185 *King.* Say to her, we have measured many miles,
To tread a measure with her on this grass.

Boyet. They say that they have measured many a mile,
To tread a measure° with you on this grass.

Rosaline. It is not so. Ask them how many inches
190   Is in one mile. If they have measured many,
The measure then of one is eas'ly told.

Boyet. If to come hither you have measured miles,
And many miles, the princess bids you tell
How many inches doth fill up one mile.

195 *Berowne.* Tell her we measure them by weary steps.

Boyet. She hears herself.

Rosaline.   How many weary steps,
Of many weary miles you have o'ergone,
Are numb'red in the travel of one mile?

Berowne. We number nothing that we spend for you.
200   Our duty is so rich, so infinite,

188 **measure** stately dance

That we may do it still without accompt.°
Vouchsafe to show the sunshine of your face,
That we like savages may worship it.

Rosaline. My face is but a moon, and clouded too.

King. Blessèd are clouds, to do as such clouds do.   205
Vouchsafe, bright moon, and these thy stars, to
shine
(Those clouds removed) upon our watery eyne.°

Rosaline. O vain petitioner, beg a greater matter!
Thou now requests but moonshine in the water.°

King. Then in our measure do but vouchsafe one
change.°   210
Thou bid'st me beg; this begging is not strange.°

Rosaline. Play, music then. Nay, you must do it soon.
[*The musicians play.*]
Not yet? No dance! Thus change I like the moon.

King. Will you not dance? How come you thus es-
trangèd?

Rosaline. You took the moon at full, but now she's
changèd.   215

King. Yet still she is the moon, and I the man.
The music plays; vouchsafe some motion to it.

Rosaline. Our ears vouchsafe it.

King.   But your legs should do it.

Rosaline. Since you are strangers and come here by
chance,
We'll not be nice.° Take hands. We will not dance.   220

King. Why take we hands then?

Rosaline.   Only to part friends.
Curtsy, sweet hearts. And so the measure ends.

---

201 **accompt** reckoning   207 **eyne** eyes   209 **moonshine in the water**
a mere nothing   210 **change** round of dancing   211 **not strange** not
unsuitably foreign   220 **nice** fastidious

King. More measure of this measure! Be not nice.

Rosaline. We can afford no more at such a price.

225 *King.* Price you yourselves. What buys your company?

Rosaline. Your absence only.

King.   That can never be.

Rosaline. Then cannot we be bought; and so adieu—
    Twice to your visor,° and half once to you.

King. If you deny to dance, let's hold more chat.

Rosaline. In private then.

230 *King.*   I am best pleased with that.
                             [They converse apart.]

Berowne. White-handed mistress, one sweet word with
    thee.

Princess. Honey, and milk, and sugar—there is three.

Berowne. Nay then, two treys,° an if° you grow so
    nice,
    Metheglin,° wort,° and malmsey.° Well run, dice!
    There's half a dozen sweets.

235 *Princess.*   Seventh sweet, adieu.
    Since you can cog,° I'll play no more with you.

Berowne. One word in secret.

Princess.   Let it not be sweet.

Berowne. Thou grievest my gall.°

Princess.   Gall! Bitter.

Berowne.   Therefore meet.°
                             [They converse apart.]

---

228 **visor** mask   233 **treys** threes (at dice)   233 **an if** if   234 **Metheglin** drink mixed with honey   234 **wort** unfermented beer   234 **malmsey** a Mediterranean wine   236 **cog** cheat   238 **gall** sore spot   238 **meet** fitting

Dumaine. Will you vouchsafe with me to change° a
    word?

Maria. Name it.

Dumaine.   Fair lady—

Maria.   Say you so? Fair lord.   *240*
  Take that for your "fair lady."

Dumaine.   Please it you,
  As much in private, and I'll bid adieu.
                    [*They converse apart.*]

Katharine. What, was your vizard° made without a
    tongue?

Longaville. I know the reason, lady, why you ask.

Katharine. O for your reason! Quickly, sir, I long.   *245*

Longaville. You have a double tongue° within your
    mask
  And would afford my speechless vizard half.

Katharine. "Veal,"° quoth the Dutchman. Is not
    "veal" a calf?

Longaville. A calf, fair lady?

Katharine.   No, a fair lord calf.

Longaville. Let's part the word.

Katharine.   No, I'll not be your half.   *250*
  Take all and wean it, it may prove an ox.

Longaville. Look how you butt yourself in these sharp
    mocks.
  Will you give horns,° chaste lady? Do not so.

Katharine. Then die a calf before your horns do grow.

Longaville. One word in private with you ere I die.   *255*

---

239 **change** exchange   243 **vizard** mask   246 **double tongue** (an inner projection or tongue held in the mouth to keep the mask in place)
248 **Veal** (Dutch or German pronunciation of "well")   253 **give horns** prove unfaithful

Katharine. Bleat softly then. The butcher hears you
    cry.   [*They converse apart.*]

Boyet. The tongues of mocking wenches are as keen
    As is the razor's edge invisible,
    Cutting a smaller hair than may be seen,
260 Above the sense° of sense; so sensible
    Seemeth their conference,° their conceits° have
        wings
    Fleeter than arrows, bullets, wind, thought, swifter
        things.

Rosaline. Not one word more, my maids, break off,
    break off.

Berowne. By heaven, all dry-beaten° with pure scoff!

265 *King.* Farewell, mad wenches. You have simple wits.
            Exeunt [*King, Lords, and Blackamoors*].

Princess. Twenty adieus, my frozen Muscovits.
    Are these the breed of wits so wondered at?

Boyet. Tapers they are, with your sweet breaths
    puffed out.

Rosaline. Well-liking° wits they have; gross, gross;
    fat, fat.

270 *Princess.* O poverty in wit, kingly-poor flout!°
    Will they not, think you, hang themselves tonight?
    Or ever but in vizards show their faces?
    This pert Berowne was out of count'nance quite.

Rosaline. They were all in lamentable cases.°
275   The king was weeping-ripe° for a good word.

Princess. Berowne did swear himself out of all suit.°

Maria. Dumaine was at my service, and his sword.
    "No point,"° quoth I; my servant straight was mute.

260 **Above the sense** above the reach   261 **conference** conferring
261 **conceits** witticisms   264 **dry-beaten** beaten with blood being
drawn   269 **Well-liking** plump, sleek   270 **kingly-poor flout** a poor
jest for a king   274 **cases** (with pun on the sense "masks" or "costumes")   275 **weeping-ripe** about to weep   276 **out of all suit** beyond all reasonableness   278 **No point** not at all

Katharine. Lord Longaville said I came o'er his heart;
    And trow° you what he called me?

Princess.   Qualm,° perhaps.   280

Katharine. Yes, in good faith.

Princess.   Go, sickness as thou art!

Rosaline. Well, better wits have worn plain statute-
    caps.°
    But will you hear? The king is my love sworn.

Princess. And quick Berowne hath plighted faith to
    me.

Katharine. And Longaville was for my service born.   285

Maria. Dumaine is mine as sure as bark on tree.

Boyet. Madam, and pretty mistresses, give ear.
    Immediately they will again be here
    In their own shapes, for it can never be
    They will digest this harsh indignity.   290

Princess. Will they return?

Boyet.   They will, they will, God knows,
    And leap for joy though they are lame with blows.
    Therefore change° favors, and when they repair,°
    Blow° like sweet roses in this summer air.

Princess. How blow? How blow? Speak to be under-
    stood.   295

Boyet. Fair ladies masked are roses in their bud;
    Dismasked, their damask° sweet commixture shown,
    Are angels vailing° clouds, or roses blown.

Princess. Avaunt, perplexity!° What shall we do
    If they return in their own shapes to woo?   300

---

280 **trow** know   280 **Qualm** sudden sickness   282 **statute-caps** caps
apprentices were required to wear   293 **change** exchange   293 **repair** come again   294 **blow** blossom   297 **damask** red and white
(like the Damascus rose)   298 **vailing** letting fall   299 **Avaunt, perplexity** away, confusion

Rosaline. Good madam, if by me you'll be advised,
    Let's mock them still, as well known as disguised.
    Let us complain to them what fools were here,
    Disguised like Muscovites in shapeless gear;°
303   And wonder what they were, and to what end
    Their shallow shows and prologue vilely penned,
    And their rough carriage so ridiculous,
    Should be presented at our tent to us.

Boyet. Ladies, withdraw. The gallants are at hand.

310 *Princess.* Whip to our tents, as roes run o'er land.
                      Exeunt [*Princess and Ladies*].

   Enter the King and the rest: [*Berowne, Longaville,*
     and Dumaine, all in their proper habits].

King. Fair sir, God save you. Where's the princess?

Boyet. Gone to her tent. Please it your Majesty
    Command me any service to her thither?

King. That she vouchsafe me audience for one word.

315 *Boyet.* I will; and so will she, I know, my lord.   *Exit.*

Berowne. This fellow pecks up wit, as pigeons peas,
    And utters it again when God doth please.
    He is wit's pedlar, and retails his wares
    At wakes° and wassails,° meetings, markets, fairs;
320   And we that sell by gross, the Lord doth know,
    Have not the grace to grace it with such show.
    This gallant pins the wenches° on his sleeve.
    Had he been Adam, he had tempted Eve.
    'A can carve° too, and lisp. Why, this is he
325   That kissed his hand away in courtesy.
    This is the ape of form,° Monsieur the Nice,°
    That, when he plays at tables,° chides the dice
    In honorable terms. Nay, he can sing

---

304 **gear** outfit   319 **wakes** vigils and feastings   319 **wassails** revelry
322 **pins the wenches** wears maidens' favors   324 **carve** make gestures of courtship   326 **form** etiquette   326 **Nice** exquisite   327 **at tables** backgammon

A mean° most meanly; and in ushering
Mend° him who can. The ladies call him sweet.　　330
The stairs, as he treads on them, kiss his feet.
This is the flow'r that smiles on every one,
To show his teeth as white as whalës-bone;
And consciences that will not die in debt
Pay him the due of "honey-tongued Boyet."　　335

King. A blister on his sweet tongue, with my heart,
That put Armado's page out of his part!

Enter [the Princess and] the Ladies [with Boyet].

Berowne. See where it comes! Behavior, what wert
thou
Till this madman showed thee, and what art thou
now?

King. All hail, sweet madam, and fair time of day.　　340

Princess. "Fair" in "all hail"° is foul, as I conceive.

King. Construe my speeches better, if you may.

Princess. Then wish me better, I will give you leave.

King. We came to visit you, and purpose now
To lead you to our court. Vouchsafe it then.　　345

Princess. This field shall hold me, and so hold your
vow.
Nor God nor I delights in perjured men.

King. Rebuke me not for that which you provoke.
The virtue° of your eye must break my oath.

Princess. You nickname° virtue. "Vice" you should
have spoke;　　350
For virtue's office never breaks men's troth.
Now, by my maiden honor, yet as pure
As the unsullied lily, I protest,

329 **mean** intermediate part　330 **Mend** surpass　341 **hail** (with a
pun on hail meaning "sleet")　349 **virtue** power　350 **nickname**
name by mistake

A world of torments though I should endure,
355 I would not yield to be your house's guest,
So much I hate a breaking cause° to be
Of heavenly oaths, vowed with integrity.

King. O, you have lived in desolation here,
Unseen, unvisited, much to our shame.

360 *Princess.* Not so, my lord. It is not so, I swear.
We have had pastimes here and pleasant game.
A mess° of Russians left us but of late.

King. How, madam? Russians?

Princess.   Ay, in truth, my lord;
Trim gallants, full of courtship and of state.

365 *Rosaline.* Madam, speak true. It is not so, my lord.
My lady, to the manner of the days,°
In courtesy gives undeserving praise.
We four indeed confronted were with four
In Russian habit.° Here they stayed an hour
370 And talked apace; and in that hour, my lord,
They did not bless us with one happy° word.
I dare not call them fools, but this I think,
When they are thirsty, fools would fain have drink.

Berowne. This jest is dry to me. Gentle sweet,
375 Your wit makes wise things foolish. When we greet
With eyes best seeing heaven's fiery eye,°
By light we lose light. Your capacity
Is of that nature that to your huge store
Wise things seem foolish and rich things but poor.

Rosaline. This proves you wise and rich, for in my
380 eye—

Berowne. I am a fool, and full of poverty.

Rosaline. But that you take what doth to you belong,
It were a fault to snatch words from my tongue.

---

356 **breaking cause** cause for breaking off   362 **mess** group of four
366 **to the manner of the days** according to the fashion of the time
369 **habit** dress   371 **happy** appropriate   376 **heaven's fiery eye** the
sun

Berowne. O, I am yours, and all that I possess.

Rosaline. All the fool mine?

Berowne.   I cannot give you less.   385

Rosaline. Which of the vizards was it that you wore?

Berowne. Where, when, what vizard? Why demand
  you this?

Rosaline. There, then, that vizard, that superfluous
  case°
  That hid the worse, and showed the better face.

King. We were descried. They'll mock us now down-
  right.   390

Dumaine. Let us confess, and turn it to a jest.

Princess. Amazed, my lord? Why looks your Highness sad?

Rosaline. Help! Hold his brows! He'll sound.° Why
  look you pale?
  Seasick, I think, coming from Muscovy.

Berowne. Thus pour the stars down plagues for per-
  jury.   395
  Can any face of brass° hold longer out?
  Here stand I, lady, dart thy skill at me.
  Bruise me with scorn, confound me with a flout,
  Thrust thy sharp wit quite through my ignorance,
  Cut me to pieces with thy keen conceit,°   400
  And I will wish thee never more to dance,
  Nor never more in Russian habit wait.
  O, never will I trust to speeches penned,
  Nor to the motion of a schoolboy's tongue,
  Nor never come in vizard to my friend,   405
  Nor woo in rhyme, like a blind harper's song!
  Taffeta phrases,° silken terms precise,
  Three-piled° hyperboles, spruce affectation,

---

388 **case** covering   393 **sound** swoon   396 **face of brass** brazen
manner   400 **conceit** imagination   407 **Taffeta phrases** fine speech
408 **Three-piled** (the finest weight velvet)

       Figures° pedantical—these summer flies

410   Have blown° me full of maggot ostentation.
       I do forswear them; and I here protest
       By this white glove (how white the hand, God
          knows!)
       Henceforth my wooing mind shall be expressed
       In russet° yeas and honest kersey° noes.

415   And to begin, wench—so God help me, law!—
       My love to thee is sound, sans° crack or flaw.

Rosaline. Sans "sans," I pray you.

Berowne.   Yet I have a trick°
       Of the old rage. Bear with me, I am sick.
       I'll leave it by degrees. Soft, let us see—

420   Write "Lord have mercy on us"° on those three.
       They are infected, in their hearts it lies;
       They have the plague, and caught it of your eyes.
       These lords are visited;° you are not free,°
       For the Lord's tokens° on you do I see.

425 *Princess.* No, they are free that gave these tokens to us.

Berowne. Our states° are forfeit. Seek not to undo us.

Rosaline. It is not so, for how can this be true,
       That you stand forfeit, being those that sue?

Berowne. Peace! for I will not have to do with you.

430 *Rosaline.* Nor shall not if I do as I intend.

Berowne. Speak for yourselves. My wit is at an end.

King. Teach us, sweet madam, for our rude transgres-
         sion
       Some fair excuse.

Princess.   The fairest is confession.
       Were not you here but even now disguised?

---

409 Figures figures of speech   **410 blown** filled   **414 russet** (characteristic red-brown color of peasants' clothes)   **414 kersey** plain wool cloth   **416 sans** without   **417 trick** trace   **420 Lord have mercy on us** (inscription posted on the doors of houses harboring the plague)   **423 visited** attacked by plague   **423 free** free of infection   **424 the Lord's tokens** plague spots   **426 states** estates

King. Madam, I was.

Princess.   And were you well advised?   435

King. I was, fair madam.

Princess.   When you then were here,
What did you whisper in your lady's ear?

King. That more than all the world I did respect her.

Princess. When she shall challenge this, you will re-
ject her.

King. Upon mine honor, no.

Princess.   Peace, peace, forbear!   440
Your oath once broke, you force not° to forswear.

King. Despise me when I break this oath of mine.

Princess. I will, and therefore keep it. Rosaline,
What did the Russian whisper in your ear?

Rosaline. Madame, he swore that he did hold me dear   445
As precious eyesight, and did value me
Above this world; adding thereto, moreover,
That he would wed me or else die my lover.

Princess. God give thee joy of him. The noble lord
Most honorably doth uphold his word.   450

King. What mean you, madam? By my life, my troth,
I never swore this lady such an oath.

Rosaline. By heaven you did! And to confirm it plain,
You gave me this, but take it, sir, again.

King. My faith and this the princess I did give.   455
I knew her by this jewel on her sleeve.

Princess. Pardon me, sir, this jewel did she wear,
And Lord Berowne, I thank him, is my dear.
What! Will you have me, or your pearl again?

Berowne. Neither of either, I remit both twain.   460
I see the trick on 't. Here was a consent,

441 **force not** do not think it wrong

Knowing aforehand of our merriment,
To dash° it like a Christmas comedy.
Some carry-tale, some please-man,° some slight
   zany,°
Some mumble-news,° some trencher-knight,° some
465   Dick°
That smiles his cheek in years,° and knows the trick
To make my lady laugh when she's disposed,
Told our intents before; which once disclosed,
The ladies did change favors, and then we,
470 Following the signs, wooed but the sign of she.
Now, to our perjury to add more terror,
We are again forsworn, in will and error.
Much upon this 'tis.° [*To Boyet*] And might not you
Forestall our sport, to make us thus untrue?
475 Do not you know my lady's foot by th' squier,°
And laugh upon the apple of her eye?°
And stand between her back, sir, and the fire,
Holding a trencher,° jesting merrily?
You put our page out.° Go, you are allowed.°
480 Die when you will, a smock° shall be your shroud.
You leer upon me, do you? There's an eye
Wounds like a leaden sword.

Boyet.   Full merrily
Hath this brave manage,° this career,° been run.

Berowne. Lo, he is tilting straight.° Peace! I have
   done.

          Enter [Costard, the] Clown.

485 Welcome, pure wit! Thou part'st a fair fray.

463 **dash** ridicule   464 **please-man** toady   464 **zany** buffoon   465
mumble-news prattler   465 **trencher-knight** brave man at the table
465 **Dick** fellow   466 **smiles his cheek in years** laughs his face into
wrinkles   473 **Much upon this 'tis** it is very much like this   475 **by
th' squier** by the rule (that is, have her measure)   476 **laugh . . .
eye** laugh, looking closely into her eyes   478 **trencher** wooden plate
479 **put our page out** take him out of his part   479 **allowed** permit-
ted (licensed, like a court fool)   480 **smock** woman's garment
483 **manage** display of horsemanship   483 **career** charge   484 **tilting straight** already jousting

Costard. O Lord, sir, they would know
　Whether the three Worthies shall come in or no.

Berowne. What, are there but three?

Costard.　　　　　　　　No, sir, but it is vara° fine,
　For every one pursents° three.

Berowne.　　　　　　And three times thrice is nine.

Costard. Not so, sir, under correction, sir, I hope, it
　is not so.　　　　　　　　　　　　　　　　　　　*490*
　You cannot beg us,° sir, I can assure you, sir; we
　　know what we know.
　I hope, sir, three times thrice, sir—

Berowne.　　　　　　　　　　Is not nine?

Costard. Under correction, sir, we know whereuntil it
　doth amount.

Berowne. By Jove, I always took three threes for nine. *495*

Costard. O Lord, sir, it were pity you should get your
　living by reck'ning, sir.

Berowne. How much is it?

Costard. O Lord, sir, the parties themselves, the ac-
　tors, sir, will show whereuntil it doth amount. For *500*
　mine own part, I am, as they say, but to parfect°
　one man in one poor man—Pompion° the Great,
　sir.

Berowne. Art thou one of the Worthies?

Costard. It pleased them to think me worthy of Pom- *505*
　pey the Great. For mine own part, I know not the
　degree° of the Worthy, but I am to stand for him.

Berowne. Go, bid them prepare.

Costard. We will turn it finely off, sir; we will take
　some care.　　　　　　　　　　　　　　　　　*Exit.*

---

488 **vara** (northern pronunciation of "very")　489 **pursents** repre-
sents　491 **beg us** prove us fools　501 **parfect** play the part of
502 **Pompion** pumpkin (for Pompey)　507 **degree** rank

King. Berowne, they will shame us. Let them not ap-
510   proach.

Berowne. We are shame-proof, my lord; and 'tis some
policy°
To have one show worse than the king's and his
company.

King. I say they shall not come.

Princess. Nay, my good lord, let me o'errule you now.
515   That sport best pleases that doth least know how,
Where zeal strives to content, and the contents
Dies in the zeal of that which it presents.°
Their form confounded makes most form in mirth°
When great things laboring perish in their birth.

520 *Berowne.* A right description of our sport, my lord.

Enter [Armado, the] Braggart.

Armado. Anointed, I implore so much expense of thy
royal sweet breath as will utter a brace° of words.
    *[Converses apart with the King, and delivers
            a paper to him.]*

Princess. Doth this man serve God?

Berowne. Why ask you?

525 *Princess.* 'A speaks not like a man of God his making.

Armado. That is all one, my fair, sweet, honey monarch; for, I protest, the schoolmaster is exceeding
fantastical; too-too vain, too-too vain; but we will
put it, as they say, to *fortuna de la guerra.*° I wish
530   you the peace of mind, most royal couplement!°
                                                    Exit.

King. Here is like to be a good presence of Worthies.

---

511 **policy** crafty device   516–17 **contents . . . presents** i.e., the
substance is destroyed by the excessive zeal in presenting it   518
Their form . . . mirth i.e., art that is confused is most laughable
entertainment   522 **brace** pair   529 **fortuna de la guerra** fortune
of war (Italian)   530 **couplement** pair

He presents Hector of Troy; the swain, Pompey the
Great; the parish curate, Alexander; Armado's page,
Hercules; the pedant, Judas Maccabaeus:
And if these four Worthies in their first show thrive,　535
These four will change habits° and present the
other five.

Berowne. There is five in the first show.

King. You are deceivèd, 'tis not so.

Berowne. The pedant, the braggart, the hedge-priest,°
the fool, and the boy—　　　　　　　　　　　540
Abate throw at novum,° and the whole world again
Cannot pick out five such, take each one in his
vein.°

King. The ship is under sail, and here she comes
amain.°

Enter [Costard, for] Pompey.

Costard. "I Pompey am—"

Berowne.　　　　　　　You lie, you are not he!

Costard. "I Pompey am—"

Boyet.　　　　　　　With libbard's head° on knee.　545

Berowne. Well said, old mocker. I must needs be
friends with thee.

Costard. "I Pompey am, Pompey surnamed the Big—"

Dumaine. The "Great."

Costard. It is "Great," sir—"Pompey surnamed the
Great,
That oft in field, with targe° and shield, did make
my foe to sweat,　　　　　　　　　　　　　　550
And traveling along this coast I here am come by
chance,

536 **habits** costumes　539 **hedge-priest** unlearned priest　541 **Abate
throw at novum** except for the throw at nine (in a game of dice)
542 **vein** characteristic way　543 **amain** swiftly　545 **libbard's head**
heraldic painting of leopard　550 **targe** shield

And lay my arms before the legs of this sweet lass
    of France."
If your ladyship would say, "Thanks, Pompey," I
    had done.

555 *Princess.* Great thanks, great Pompey.

Costard. 'Tis not so much worth, but I hope I was
    perfect. I made a little fault in "Great."

Berowne. My hat to a halfpenny, Pompey proves the
    best Worthy.

Enter [Nathaniel, the] Curate, for Alexander.

Nathaniel. "When in the world I lived, I was the
560   world's commander;
    By east, west, north, and south, I spread my con-
        quering might;
    My scutcheon° plain declares that I am Alis-
        ander—"

Boyet. Your nose says, no, you are not; for it stands
    too right.°

Berowne. Your nose smells "no" in this, most tender-
    smelling knight.

Princess. The conqueror is dismayed. Proceed, good
565   Alexander.

Nathaniel. "When in the world I lived, I was the
    world's commander—"

Boyet. Most true, 'tis right—you were so, Alisander.

Berowne. Pompey the Great—

Costard. Your servant, and Costard.

570 *Berowne.* Take away the conqueror, take away Alis-
    ander.

Costard. [*To Nathaniel*] O, sir, you have overthrown

562 **scutcheon** coat of arms   563 **right** straight (Alexander's neck
was a little awry)

Alisander the conqueror! You will be scraped out
of the painted cloth° for this. Your lion that holds
his pole-ax° sitting on a close-stool° will be given 575
to Ajax.° He will be the ninth Worthy. A conqueror, and afeard to speak? Run away for shame,
Alisander. [*Nathaniel stands aside.*] There, an 't°
shall please you, a foolish mild man; an honest
man, look you, and soon dashed. He is a marvelous 580
good neighbor, faith, and a very good bowler; but
for Alisander—alas! you see how 'tis—a little o'erparted.° But there are Worthies a-coming will speak
their mind in some other sort.

Princess. Stand aside, good Pompey. 585
                          [*Costard stands aside.*]

    Enter [Holofernes, the] Pedant, for Judas, and
        [Moth,] the Boy, for Hercules.

Holofernes. "Great Hercules is presented by this imp,°
  Whose club killed Cerberus, that three-headed
    canus;°
  And when he was a babe, a child, a shrimp,
  Thus did he strangle serpents in his *manus.*°
  Quoniam° he seemeth in minority,° 590
  Ergo° I come with this apology."
  Keep some state° in thy exit, and vanish.
                       Exit Boy [*to one side*].
  "Judas I am—"

Dumaine. A Judas?

Holofernes. Not Iscariot, sir. 595
  "Judas I am, ycleped° Maccabaeus."°

Dumaine. Judas Maccabaeus clipt° is plain Judas.

574 **painted cloth** wall-hanging 575 **pole-ax** battle-ax (and penis)
575 **close-stool** commode 576 **Ajax** Greek warrior (with a pun on
"jakes," privy) 578 **an't** if it 582–83 **o'erparted** having too difficult a part 586 **imp** child 587 **canus** (from Latin *canis*) dog
589 **manus** hand 590 **Quoniam** since 590 **in minority** under age
591 **Ergo** therefore 592 **state** dignity 596 **ycleped** called 596
Maccabaeus Hebrew warrior 597 **clipt** (1) cut (2) embraced

Berowne. A kissing traitor. How, art thou proved Judas?

600 *Holofernes.* "Judas I am—"

Dumaine. The more shame for you, Judas.

Holofernes. What mean you, sir?

Boyet. To make Judas hang himself.

Holofernes. Begin, sir; you are my elder.

605 *Berowne.* Well followed: Judas was hanged on an elder.°

Holofernes. I will not be put out of countenance.

Berowne. Because thou hast no face.

Holofernes. What is this?

610 *Boyet.* A cittern-head.°

Dumaine. The head of a bodkin.°

Berowne. A death's face in a ring.°

Longaville. The face of an old Roman coin, scarce seen.

615 *Boyet.* The pommel of Caesar's falchion.°

Dumaine. The carved-bone face on a flask.

Berowne. Saint George's half-cheek° in a brooch.

Dumaine. Ay, and in a brooch of lead.°

Berowne. Ay, and worn in the cap of a toothdrawer.
620   And now forward, for we have put thee in countenance.

Holofernes. You have put me out of countenance.°

---

606 **elder** a kind of tree   610 **cittern-head** head of a stringed musical instrument   611 **bodkin** long hairpin   612 **death's face in a ring** finger ring with the carving of a skull   615 **falchion** sword   617 **half-cheek** profile   618 **brooch of lead** ornament worn in cap as badge of dentist's trade   622 **out of countenance** disconcerted

Berowne. False. We have given thee faces.

Holofernes. But you have outfaced them all.

Berowne. And° thou wert a lion, we would do so.　　625

Boyet. Therefore as he is an ass, let him go.
And so adieu, sweet Jude. Nay, why dost thou stay?

Dumaine. For the latter end of his name.

Berowne. For the ass to the Jude? Give it him. Jud-as,
away!

Holofernes. This is not generous, not gentle, not humble.　　630

Boyet. A light for Monsieur Judas! It grows dark, he
may stumble.　　　　　　*[Holofernes stands aside.]*

Princess. Alas, poor Maccabaeus, how hath he been
baited!°

Enter [Armado, the] Braggart, [for Hector].

Berowne. Hide thy head, Achilles! Here comes Hec-
tor° in arms.

Dumaine. Though my mocks come home by me, I　635
will now be merry.

King. Hector was but a Troyan in respect of this.

Boyet. But is this Hector?

King. I think Hector was not so clean-timbered.°

Longaville. His leg is too big for Hector's.　　640

Dumaine. More calf, certain.

Boyet. No; he is best indued in the small.°

Berowne. This cannot be Hector.

Dumaine. He's a god or a painter; for he makes faces.

625 **And** if　632 **baited** tormented　633–34 **Achilles . . . Hector**
(the Greek and Trojan champions)　639 **clean-timbered** clean-
limbed　642 **small** lower part of the leg

Armado. "The armipotent° Mars, of lances the al-
645   mighty,
    Gave Hector a gift—"

Dumaine. A gilt nutmeg.°

Berowne. A lemon.

Longaville. Stuck with cloves.

650 *Dumaine.* No, cloven.

Armado. Peace!
    "The armipotent Mars, of lances the almighty,
    Gave Hector a gift, the heir of Ilion;
    A man so breathed° that certain he would fight, yea
655   From morn till night, out of his pavilion.°
    I am that flower—"

Dumaine.   That mint.

Longaville.   That columbine.

Armado. Sweet Lord Longaville, rein thy tongue.

Longaville. I must rather give it the rein, for it runs
    against Hector.

660 *Dumaine.* Ay, and Hector's a greyhound.

Armado. The sweet war-man is dead and rotten.
    Sweet chucks, beat not the bones of the buried.
    When he breathed, he was a man. But I will for-
    ward with my device. [*To the Princess*] Sweet roy-
665   alty, bestow on me the sense of hearing.
             Berowne steps forth [*to whisper to Costard*].

Princess. Speak, brave Hector; we are much delighted.

Armado. I do adore thy sweet Grace's slipper.

Boyet. [*Aside to Dumaine*] Loves her by the foot.

Dumaine. [*Aside to Boyet*] He may not by the yard.°

---

645 **armipotent** powerful in arms   647 **gilt nutmeg** (with special
icing)   654 **breathed** well-exercised   655 **pavilion** tent for a cham-
pion at a tournament   669 **yard** (slang word for male organ)

Armado. "This Hector far surmounted Hannibal—"   *670*
The party is gone.°

Costard. Fellow Hector, she is gone.° She is two
months on her way.

Armado. What meanest thou?

Costard. Faith, unless you play the honest Troyan,   *675*
the poor wench is cast away. She's quick;° the child
brags in her belly already. 'Tis yours.

Armado. Dost thou infamonize° me among poten-
tates? Thou shalt die.

Costard. Then shall Hector be whipped for Jaquenetta   *680*
that is quick by him, and hanged for Pompey that
is dead by him.

Dumaine. Most rare Pompey!

Boyet. Renowned Pompey!

Berowne. Greater than great. Great, great, great Pom-   *685*
pey! Pompey the Huge!

Dumaine. Hector trembles.

Berowne. Pompey is moved. More Ates,° more Ates!
Stir them on, stir them on!

Dumaine. Hector will challenge him.   *690*

Berowne. Ay, if 'a have no more man's blood in his
belly than will sup a flea.

Armado. By the North Pole, I do challenge thee.

Costard. I will not fight with a pole, like a northern
man. I'll slash; I'll do it by the sword. I bepray   *695*
you, let me borrow my arms again.

Dumaine. Room for the incensed Worthies!

Costard. I'll do it in my shirt.

---

671 **The party is gone** (referring to Hector)   672 **she is gone** she is
pregnant   676 **quick** pregnant   678 **infamonize** defame   688 **Ates**
goddess of mischief

Dumaine. Most resolute Pompey!

700 *Moth.* Master, let me take you a buttonhole lower.° Do you not see, Pompey is uncasing° for the combat? What mean you? You will lose your reputation.

Armado. Gentlemen and soldiers, pardon me. I will 705 not combat in my shirt.

Dumaine. You may not deny it. Pompey hath made the challenge.

Armado. Sweet bloods, I both may and will.

Berowne. What reason have you for 't?

710 *Armado.* The naked truth of it is, I have no shirt. I go woolward° for penance.

Boyet. True, and it was enjoined° him in Rome for want of linen; since when, I'll be sworn he wore none but a dishclout of Jaquenetta's, and that 'a 715 wears next his heart for a favor.

Enter a Messenger, Monsieur Marcade.

Marcade. God save you, madam.

Princess. Welcome, Marcade,
But that thou interrupt'st our merriment.

Marcade. I am sorry, madam, for the news I bring 720 Is heavy in my tongue. The king your father—

Princess. Dead, for my life!

Marcade. Even so. My tale is told.

Berowne. Worthies, away! The scene begins to cloud.

Armado. For mine own part, I breathe free breath.

---

700 **take you a buttonhole lower** take you down a peg   701 **uncasing** removing his coat   711 **go woolward** wearing wool next to the skin 712 **enjoined** commanded

I have seen the day of wrong through the little hole *725*
of discretion, and I will right myself like a soldier.
                            Exeunt Worthies.

King. How fares your Majesty?

Princess. Boyet, prepare. I will away tonight.

King. Madam, not so. I do beseech you, stay.

Princess. Prepare, I say. I thank you, gracious lords, *730*
For all your fair endeavors, and entreat
Out of a new-sad soul that you vouchsafe
In your rich wisdom to excuse, or hide
The liberal opposition of our spirits,
If over-boldly we have borne ourselves *735*
In the converse of breath.° Your gentleness
Was guilty of it. Farewell, worthy lord.
A heavy heart bears not a humble° tongue.
Excuse me so, coming too short of thanks
For my great suit so easily obtained. *740*

King. The extreme parts of time extremely forms
All causes to the purpose of his speed,°
And often at his very loose° decides
That which long process could not arbitrate.
And though the mourning brow of progeny° *745*
Forbid the smiling courtesy of love
The holy suit which fain it would convince,°
Yet, since love's argument was first on foot,
Let not the cloud of sorrow justle it
From what it purposed; since to wail friends lost *750*
Is not by much so wholesome-profitable
As to rejoice at friends but newly found.

Princess. I understand you not. My griefs are double.

Berowne. Honest plain words best pierce the ear of
    grief;
And by these badges° understand the king. *755*

736 **converse of breath** conversation   738 **humble** i.e., civil, tactful
741–42 **The extreme . . . speed** time, as it runs out, directs everything
towards its conclusion   743 **at his very loose** in the act of letting go
745 **progeny** descendants   747 **convince** prove   755 **badges** tokens

For your fair sakes have we neglected time,
Played foul play with our oaths. Your beauty,
        ladies,
Hath much deformed us, fashioning our humors
Even to the opposèd end of our intents;
760 And what in us hath seemed ridiculous—
As love is full of unbefitting strains,
All wanton as a child, skipping and vain,
Formed by the eye and therefore, like the eye,
Full of straying shapes, of habits and of forms,
765 Varying in subjects as the eye doth roll
To every varied object in his glance;
Which parti-coated° presence of loose love
Put on by us, if, in your heavenly eyes,
Have misbecomed our oaths and gravities,
770 Those heavenly eyes that look into these faults
Suggested° us to make. Therefore, ladies,
Our love being yours, the error that love makes
Is likewise yours. We to ourselves prove false,
By being once false forever to be true
775 To those that make us both—fair ladies, you.
And even that falsehood, in itself a sin,
Thus purifies itself and turns to grace.

Princess. We have received your letters, full of love;
Your favors, the ambassadors of love;
780 And in our maiden council rated° them
At courtship, pleasant jest, and courtesy,
As bombast° and as lining to the time.
But more devout than this in our respects
Have we not been, and therefore met your loves
785 In their own fashion, like a merriment.

Dumaine. Our letters, madam, showed much more
        than jest.

Longaville. So did our looks.

Rosaline.   We did not quote° them so.

---

767 **parti-coated** fool's motley   771 **Suggested** tempted   780 **rated**
valued   782 **bombast** padding   787 **quote** regard

King. Now, at the latest minute of the hour
  Grant us your loves.

Princess.   A time, methinks, too short
  To make a world-without-end bargain in.   *790*
  No, no, my lord, your Grace is perjured much,
  Full of dear guiltiness; and therefore this—
  If for my love (as there is no such cause)
  You will do aught, this shall you do for me:
  Your oath I will not trust, but go with speed   *795*
  To some forlorn and naked hermitage,
  Remote from all the pleasures of the world;
  There stay until the twelve celestial signs°
  Have brought about the annual reckoning.
  If this austere insociable life   *800*
  Change not your offer made in heat of blood—
  If frosts and fasts, hard lodging and thin weeds,°
  Nip not the gaudy blossoms of your love,
  But that it bear this trial, and last love—
  Then, at the expiration of the year,   *805*
  Come challenge me, challenge me by these deserts,
  And, by this virgin palm now kissing thine,
  I will be thine; and till that instant, shut
  My woeful self up in a mourning house,
  Raining the tears of lamentation   *810*
  For the remembrance of my father's death.
  If this thou do deny, let our hands part,
  Neither entitled in the other's heart.

King. If this, or more than this, I would deny,
  To flatter up° these powers of mine with rest,   *815*
  The sudden hand of death close up mine eye!
  Hence hermit then—my heart is in thy breast.

[*Berowne.* And what to me, my love? and what to me?

Rosaline. You must be purgèd, too, your sins are
      rank,
  You are attaint° with faults and perjury;   *820*

---

798 **twelve celestial signs** (of the Zodiac)   802 **weeds** garments   815
flatter up pamper   820 **attaint** charged

Therefore, if you my favor mean to get,
A twelvemonth shall you spend, and never rest,
But seek the weary beds of people sick.]°

Dumaine. But what to me, my love? But what to me?
825   A wife?

Katharine.   A beard, fair health, and honesty;
With three-fold love I wish you all these three.

Dumaine. O, shall I say "I thank you, gentle wife"?

Katharine. Not so, my lord. A twelvemonth and a day
I'll mark no words that smooth-faced wooers say.
830   Come when the king doth to my lady come;
Then, if I have much love, I'll give you some.

Dumaine. I'll serve thee true and faithfully till then.

Katharine. Yet swear not, lest ye be forsworn again.

Longaville. What says Maria?

Maria.   At the twelvemonth's end
835   I'll change my black gown for a faithful friend.

Longaville. I'll stay with patience, but the time is long.

Maria. The liker° you! Few taller are so young.

Berowne. Studies my lady? Mistress, look on me.
Behold the window of my heart, mine eye,
840   What humble suit attends thy answer there.
Impose some service on me for thy love.

Rosaline. Oft have I heard of you, my Lord Berowne,
Before I saw you, and the world's large tongue
Proclaims you for a man replete with mocks,
845   Full of comparisons and wounding flouts,°
Which you on all estates° will execute
That lie within the mercy of your wit.

818–23 (lines 824–35) duplicate this passage in an expanded form;
probably Shakespeare failed to indicate clearly that these six lines
had been superseded)   837 **liker** more like   845 **wounding flouts**
painful jokes   846 **all estates** men of all kinds

To weed this wormwood° from your fructful° brain,
And therewithal to win me, if you please,
Without the which I am not to be won,   *850*
You shall this twelvemonth term from day to day
Visit the speechless sick, and still° converse
With groaning wretches; and your task shall be
With all the fierce endeavor of your wit
To enforce the painèd impotent to smile.   *855*

Berowne. To move wild laughter in the throat of
   death?
It cannot be; it is impossible;
Mirth cannot move a soul in agony.

Rosaline. Why, that's the way to choke a gibing spirit,
Whose influence is begot of that loose grace   *860*
Which shallow laughing hearers give to fools.
A jest's prosperity lies in the ear
Of him that hears it, never in the tongue
Of him that makes it. Then, if sickly ears,
Deafed with the clamors of their own dear groans,   *865*
Will hear your idle scorns, continue then,
And I will have you and that fault withal;
But if they will not, throw away that spirit,
And I shall find you empty of that fault,
Right joyful of your reformation.   *870*

Berowne. A twelvemonth? Well, befall what will befall,
I'll jest a twelvemonth in an hospital.

Princess. [*To the King*] Ay, sweet my lord, and so I
   take my leave.

King. No, madam, we will bring you on your way.

Berowne. Our wooing doth not end like an old play;   *875*
Jack hath not Jill. These ladies' courtesy
Might well have made our sport a comedy.

---

848 **wormwood** bitterness   848 **fructful** fruitful   852 **still** always

King. Come, sir, it wants a twelvemonth and a day,
And then 'twill end.

Berowne.   That's too long for a play.

Enter [Armado, the] Braggart.

880 *Armado.* Sweet Majesty, vouchsafe me—

Princess. Was not that Hector?

Dumaine. The worthy knight of Troy.

Armado. I will kiss thy royal finger, and take leave.
I am a votary;° I have vowed to Jaquenetta to hold
885 the plough for her sweet love three year. But, most
esteemed greatness, will you hear the dialogue that
the two learned men have compiled in praise of the
owl and the cuckoo? It should have followed in
the end of our show.

890 *King.* Call them forth quickly; we will do so.

Armado. Holla! Approach.

Enter all.

This side is *Hiems,* Winter; this *Ver,* the Spring;
the one maintained by the owl, th' other by the
cuckoo. *Ver,* begin.

The Song.

895 [*Spring.*]   When daisies pied° and violets blue
            And lady-smocks° all silver-white
        And cuckoo-buds° of yellow hue
            Do paint the meadows with delight,

---

884 **votary** sworn follower   895 **pied** parti-colored   896 **lady-smocks**
water-cresses, or cuckoo flowers   897 **cuckoo-buds** crowfoot, or
buttercup

The cuckoo then, on every tree,
Mocks married men; for thus sings he,   *900*
                          "Cuckoo!
Cuckoo, cuckoo!" O word of fear,
Unpleasing to a married ear!
When shepherds pipe on oaten straws,
    And merry larks are ploughmen's
                          clocks,   *905*
When turtles tread,° and rooks, and daws,
    And maidens bleach their summer
                          smocks,
The cuckoo then, on every tree,
Mocks married men; for thus sings he,
                          "Cuckoo!   *910*
Cuckoo, cuckoo!" O word of fear,
Unpleasing to a married ear!

Winter.   When icicles hang by the wall,
    And Dick the shepherd blows his nail,°
And Tom bears logs into the hall,   *915*
    And milk comes frozen home in pail,
When blood is nipped, and ways be foul,
Then nightly sings the staring owl,
                          "Tu-whit,
Tu-who!" a merry note,   *920*
While greasy Joan doth keel° the pot.

When all aloud the wind doth blow,
    And coughing drowns the parson's
                          saw,°
And birds sit brooding in the snow,
    And Marian's nose looks red and raw,   *925*
When roasted crabs° hiss in the bowl,
Then nightly sings the staring owl,
                          "Tu-whit,

---

906 **turtles tread** turtledoves mate   914 **blows his nail** blows on his
fingernails to warm them (and so, waiting patiently)   921 **keel** cool,
by stirring or skimming   923 **saw** wise saying   926 **crabs** crab
apples

Tu-who!" a merry note,
930   While greasy Joan doth keel the pot.

[*Armado*.] The words of Mercury are harsh after the
songs of Apollo.° [You that way, we this way.
                                        Exeunt omnes.]

                         FINIS

931–32 **The words ... Apollo** i.e., let us end with the songs, because
clever words of the god Mercury would come harshly after the songs
of Apollo, the god of poetry

Textual Note

This edition is based upon the quarto of 1598, which, it is generally agreed, was printed from a manuscript in Shakespeare's own hand. The title page reads: "A / Pleasant / Conceited Comedie / Called, / Loues labors lost. / As it was presented before her Highnes / this last Christmas. / Newly corrected and augmented / By W. Shakespere. / Imprinted at London by W. W. / for Cutbert Burby. / 1598."

Although here there may be a reference to a previous printing, there is no trace of an earlier edition. "Newly corrected and augmented" probably refers to revisions in the manuscript, some of which, as it happens, may be detected in examining the printed text. (See footnotes at IV.iii.295 and V.ii.818–23.)

The printing of the 1623 Folio is based upon the quarto. It corrects some errors of the quarto and adds a number of its own. It provides act divisions (mistakenly heading the fifth act "Actus Quartus"), but the scene divisions as well as the list of the names of the persons in the play are the contributions of later editors.

Apart from a considerable number of misreadings the most noteworthy confusions in the quarto are in the speech headings. It is not merely that occasionally *Nathaniel* stands for *Holofernes*, that the *King* is sometimes *Navarre* and sometimes *Ferdinand* in the early part of the second act, and that in the same part of the play Rosaline and Katharine are confused. In the next act the character previously identified as Armado becomes

"Braggart," Moth, the Page, becomes "Boy," Holofernes becomes "Pedant," Costard becomes "Clown." Later Sir Nathaniel becomes "Curate" and "Constable" becomes "Dull." The use of the generic names to take the place of the individual ones may be evidence of Shakespeare's revisions. In the present edition the speech headings have been made consistent, but the later substitutions are made evident by the supplementary stage directions indicating the entrances of the various characters.

The revision of the manuscript has left a couple of other obvious confusions. Berowne's speech in Act IV, Scene iii contains lines that belong to an earlier version, and some of these should have been canceled. If lines 295–316 were omitted, the speech would continue connectedly and without obvious repetitions. It also seems that the exchange between Berowne and Rosaline in Act V, Scene ii, lines 818–23, was meant to be struck out. In the present edition these passages are retained, but enclosed in square brackets.

The text of this edition is based upon the Heber-Daniel copy of the quarto in the British Museum; the spelling and punctuation have been modernized, obvious misspellings and wrong speech headings corrected, and the quotations from foreign languages regularized. Other departures from the quarto text are listed below: the adopted reading is given first, in italics, followed immediately by the quarto reading in roman letters.

I.i.24 *three* thee   31 *pomp* pome   62 *feast* fast   104 *an* any   114 *swore* sworne   127–31 [Q gives to Longaville]   127 *gentility* gentletie   130 *public* publibue   131 *possibly* possible   218 *welkin's vicegerent* welkis Vizgerent   240 *preposterous* propostrous   276 *worst* wost   289 *King* Ber.   308–09 *prosperity* prosperie

I.ii.14 *epitheton* apethaton   100 *blushing* blush-in   143 *Dull* Clo.

II.i.32 *Importunes* Importuous   34 *visaged* visage   44 *parts* peerelsse   88 *unpeopled* vnpeeled   115–26 [the lines here given to Rosaline are in Q given to Katharine]   130 *half of an* halfe of, of an   140 *friendship* faiendship   142 *demand* pemaund   144 *On* One   179 *mine own* my none   195 *Katharine* Rosalin   210 *Rosaline* Katherin   221 [Q gives to *La.*]   222–23 [Q gives to *Lad.*]   224 [Q gives to *La.*]   236 *agate* Agot   246 *quote* coate   254 [Q gives to

Lad.] 255 [Q gives to *Lad.* 2] 256 [Q gives to *Lad.* 3] 257 [Q gives to *Lad.*] 258 [Q gives to *Lad.*]

III.i.14 *throat as if* throate, if 16 *through the nose* through: nose 19 *thin-belly* thinbellies 25 *note me?—that* note men that 28 *penny* penne 67 *voluble* volable 74 *the mail* thee male 74 *plain* pline 136 *ounce* ouce 139 *remuneration* remuration 140 *One penny* i.d. 177 *beadle* Bedell 178 *critic* Crietick 182 *senior-junior* signior *Iunios* 186 *plackets* Placcats 188 *paritors* Parrators 192 *German clock* Iermane Cloake 198 *whitely* whitly 206 *sue* shue

IV.i.6 *On* Ore 33 *heart* hart 71 *saw ... saw* See ... see 72 *overcame* couercame 76 *king's* King 110 *suitor ... suitor* shooter ... shooter 122 *Pepin* Pippen 125 *Guinever* Guinouer 132 *hit it* hit 134 *mete* meate 136 *ne'er* neare 138 *pin* is in 140 *too* to 146 *to th' one* ath toothen 149 *o' t'* other atother 150 *a* most most 150 s.d. *Shout* Shoot 151 *Exit* Exeunt

IV.ii.5 *coelo* Celo 8 *epithets* epythithes 30 *we of taste* we taste 31 *indiscreet* indistreell 37 *Dictynna ... Dictynna* Dictisima ... dictisima 38 *Dictynna* dictima 52 *ignorant, I call* ignorault cald 55 *scurrility* squirilitie 57 *preyful* prayfull 61 *sores o' sorel* sores o sorell 66–150 [all speech prefixes of Holofernes and Nathaniel are reversed in Q, except at 107] 70 *pia mater* primater 72 *those in whom* those whom 78 *ingenious* ingenous 80 *sapit* sapis 84 *pierce-one* Person 86 *likest* liklest 94–95 *Fauste . . . ruminat* Facile precor gellida, quando pecas omnia sub vmbra ruminat 98–99 *Venetia ... pretia* vemchie, vencha, que non te vnde, que non te perreche 122 *canzonet* cangenet 136 *writing* written 138 *Sir Nathaniel* Ped. Sir Holofernes 159 *ben* bien

IV.iii.13,14 *melancholy* mallicholie 48 *King* Long. 52 *triumviry* triumpherie 74 *idolatry* ydotarie 86 *quoted* coted 92 *And I mine* And mine 98 *ode* Odo 107 *Wished* Wish 111 *thorn* throne 129 *o'erheard* ore-hard 154 *coaches* couches 160 *mote ... mote* Moth ... Moth 179 *men like you, men* men men like men 181 *Joan* Ione 247 *wood* word 258 *painting and usurping* painting vsurping 259 *doters* dooters 312 *woman's* womas 315–16 [between these lines Q has: With our selues] 322 *beauty's* beautis 358 *authors* authour 360 *Let us* Lets vs 382 *Allons!* *Allons!* Alone alone 384 *forsworn* forsorne

V.i.10 *hominem* hominum 28 *insanie* infamie 30 *bone* bene 31 *Bone? Bone for bene!* *Priscian* Bome boon for boon prescian 34 *gaudeo* gaudio 36 *Quare* Quari 51 *pueritia* puericia 52 *silly* seely 59 *wave* wane 59 *Mediterranean* meditaranium 60 *venew* vene we 69 *manu* vnū 78 *dunghill* dungil 79 *Dunghill* dunghel 99 *importunate* importunt 110 *secrecy* secretie 119 *Nathaniel* Holofernes 121 *rend'red* rended 153 *Allons* Alone

V.ii.13 *ne'er* neare   17 *ha' been a grandam* a bin Grandam   43
'Ware pencils, ho! Ware pensalls, How?   53 *pearls* Pearle   65 *hests*
deuice   74 *wantonness* wantons be   80 *stabbed* stable   89 *syca-*
more Siccamone   93 *Warily* warely   95 *overheard* ouer hard   96
they thy   122 *parley, court* parlee, to court   134 *too* two   148 *her*
his   152 *e'er* ere   159 [Q gives to Berowne]   163 *ever* euen   175
strangers stranges   217 [Q gives to Rosaline]   225 *Price* Prise
243–56 [Q gives "Maria" for "Katharine"]   298 *vailing* varling   300
woo woe   310 *run* runs   324 *too* to   329 *ushering* hushering   342
Construe Consture   353 *unsullied* vnsallied   375 *wit* wits   408 *af-*
fectation affection   461 *on't* ant   464 *zany* saine   483 *manage*
nuage   501 *they* thy   515 *least* best   529 *de la guerra* delaguar
564 *this* his   584 [Q has "Exit Curat"]   598 *proved* proud   647
gilt gift   689 *Stir them on, stir* stir stir them, or stir   751 *wholesome*
holdsome   779 *the ambassadors* embassadours   783 *this in our* this
our   787 *quote* cote   808 *instant* instance   813 *entitled* intiled
817 *hermit* herrite   819 *rank* rackt   825 *A wife?* [included in following speech in Q]   829 *smoothed-faced* smothfast   896–97
[these lines transposed in Q]   917 *foul* full   931–32 *The words ...*
Apollo [printed in larger type in Q without any speech-heading; F
adds *You that way: we this way,* and heading *Brag.*]

A Note on the Sources of
Love's Labor's Lost

No source for the plot of *Love's Labor's Lost* is known to exist but it is often supposed that Shakespeare was building upon reports of historic events. The very names of Navarre and the lords,[1] the matter of property disputes involving the King of France, the existence of a learned academy favored by the French nobility, and accounts of political negotiations in which certain court ladies were involved, all these point to incidents in recent French history which were reported upon at the time. So far no record has been found of any single happening that is plainly the original of the episodes of the play. It is only in the sum of the reports of similar incidents that the idea that Shakespeare is building upon historical matters comes to seem truly likely.

The play, whether meant originally for performance at a great house, or at a children's theater, exploited these historical events presumably because they treated matters in which the audience was also interested. English court circles were also drawn to the idea of learned academies and were involved in disputes centering on Platonic theories of love. Upon reflection, the treatment of certain episodes in France would have served as comment upon the life of the court in England. Quite as naturally Shake-

[1] The Marshall de Biron (Berowne) and Longueville were close associates of Henry, not Ferdinand, of Navarre. The Duc de Mayenne (Dumaine?) was once his enemy but later an ally. Boyet and Marcadé are the names of historical persons.

speare could work into the main story all sorts of allusions
to the life of letters and introduce subsidiary plotting to
expand upon the story of the aristocratic academicians.
So the play directs particular satire against specific English fashions—euphuism, for instance—as well as the
universal extravagances of humanists and pedants and
actors. Here, too, the references seem again and again to
point to particular persons and to specific incidents, and
scholars have therefore argued that Shakespeare took
some of his contemporaries as models for the characters
in his comic plot, and the characters that were in part
borrowed from the *commedia dell'arte* from time to time
present themselves in the guise of Thomas Nashe, Sir
Walter Raleigh, John Florio, and perhaps others. To J. D.
Wilson these matters become so important that he is
convinced that the play "was written as a *topical* play."
But G. L. Kittredge, and others after him, have thought
it "merely whimsical" to identify Armado and Holofernes
and the others in any such way.

On particular points it is seldom possible to resolve
this dispute, most especially if the supposed allusions are
studied primarily in the light of literary history. But the
direction of much modern literary scholarship is to give
precedence in the consideration of the elements of a work
of art to a study of their relation to the work itself as
an imaginative entity, and the effect of such an emphasis
is to work in opposition to any theory that regards the
work primarily as a historical record. In short, the impression of topical allusion is inescapable, but if one takes
the play as substantially summed up by its title, the topicality seems to be absorbed in the imaginative and the
fanciful, and in all the charm of the play's poetic and
theatrical effects.

The historical documents that are most often cited in
presenting analogues to certain incidents in the play are:
The Chronicles of Enguerrand de Monstrelet, 1440–1516;
Pierre de la Primaudaye, *The French Academie;* H. C.
Davila, *The History of the Civil Wars of France; Gesta
Grayorum: or The History of the High and Mighty Prince
Henry, Prince of Purpoole . . . who Reigned and Died,*

A. D. 1594. The relevant sections can be found in the first volume of Geoffrey Bullough's *Narrative and Dramatic Sources of Shakespeare*. There are of course no documents that in any substantial way support the ascriptions of topicality.

Commentaries

from *Appreciations*

Love's Labors Lost is one of the earliest of Shakespeare's dramas, and has many of the peculiarities of his poems, which are also the work of his earlier life. The opening speech of the king on the immortality of fame —on the triumph of fame over death—and the nobler parts of Biron, display something of the monumental style of Shakespeare's sonnets, and are not without their conceits of thought and expression. This connection of *Love's Labors Lost* with Shakespeare's poems is further enforced by the actual insertion in it of three sonnets and a faultless song; which, in accordance with his practice in other plays, are inwoven into the argument of the piece and, like the golden ornaments of a fair woman, give it a peculiar air of distinction. There is merriment in it also, with choice illustrations of both wit and humor; a laughter, often exquisite, ringing, if faintly, yet as genuine laughter still, though sometimes sinking into mere

From *Appreciations* by Walter Pater. London and New York: The Macmillan Company, 1889. The essay was first published in *Macmillan's Magazine*, December, 1885.

burlesque, which has not lasted quite so well. And Shakespeare brings a serious effect out of the trifling of his characters. A dainty lovemaking is interchanged with the more cumbrous play: below the many artifices of Biron's amorous speeches we may trace sometimes the "unutterable longing"; and the lines in which Katherine describes the blighting through love of her younger sister are one of the most touching things in older literature.[1] Again, how many echoes seem awakened by those strange words, actually said in jest!—"The sweet war-man (Hector of Troy) is dead and rotten; sweet chucks, beat not the bones of the buried: when he breathed, he was a man!" —words which may remind us of Shakespeare's own epitaph. In the last scene, an ingenious turn is given to the action, so that the piece does not conclude after the manner of other comedies.—

> Our wooing doth not end like an old play;
> Jack hath not Jill:

and Shakespeare strikes a passionate note across it at last, in the entrance of the messenger, who announces to the princess that the king her father is suddenly dead.

The merely dramatic interest of the piece is slight enough; only just sufficient, indeed, to form the vehicle of its wit and poetry. The scene—a park of the King of Navarre—is unaltered throughout; and the unity of the play is not so much the unity of a drama as that of a series of pictorial groups, in which the same figures reappear, in different combinations but on the same background. It is as if Shakespeare had intended to bind together, by some inventive conceit, the devices of an ancient tapestry, and give voices to its figures. On one side, a fair palace; on the other, the tents of the Princess of France, who has come on an embassy from her father to the King of Navarre; in the midst, a wide space of smooth grass. The same personages are combined over and over again into a series of gallant scenes: the princess, the three masked ladies, the quaint, pedantic king—

[1] Act V. Scene II.

one of those amiable kings men have never loved enough,
whose serious occupation with the things of the mind
seems, by contrast with the more usual forms of kingship,
like frivolity or play. Some of the figures are grotesque
merely, and all the male ones at least, a little fantastic.
Certain objects reappearing from scene to scene—love
letters crammed with verses to the margin, and lovers'
toys—hint obscurely at some story of intrigue. Between
these groups, on a smaller scale, come the slighter and
more homely episodes, with Sir Nathaniel the curate, the
country-maid Jaquenetta, Moth or Mote the elfin-page,
with Hiems and Ver, who recite "the dialogue that the
two learned men have compiled in praise of the owl and
the cuckoo." The ladies are lodged in tents, because the
king, like the princess of the modern poet's fancy, has
taken a vow

To make his court a little Academe,

and for three years' space no woman may come within
a mile of it; and the play shows how this artificial attempt
was broken through. For the king and his three fellow
scholars are of course soon forsworn, and turn to writing
sonnets, each to his chosen lady. These fellow scholars
of the king—"quaint votaries of science" at first, after-
wards "affection's men-at-arms"—three youthful knights,
gallant, amorous, chivalrous, but also a little affected,
sporting always a curious foppery of language, are,
throughout, the leading figures in the foreground; one of
them, in particular, being more carefully depicted than
the others, and in himself very noticeable—a portrait
with somewhat puzzling manner and expression, which
at once catches the eye irresistibly and keeps it fixed.

Play is often that about which people are most serious;
and the humorist may observe how, under all love of
playthings, there is almost always hidden an appreciation
of something really engaging and delightful. This is true
always of the toys of children: it is often true of the playthings of grown-up people, their vanities, their fopperies
even, their lighter loves; the cynic would add their pur-

suit of fame. Certainly, this is true without exception of
the playthings of a past age, which to those who succeed it are always full of a pensive interest—old manners,
old dresses, old houses. For what is called fashion in these
matters occupies, in each age, much of the care of many
of the most discerning people, furnishing them with a
kind of mirror of their real inward refinements and their
capacity for selection. Such modes or fashions are, at their
best, an example of the artistic predominance of form
over matter—of the manner of the doing of it over the
thing done—and have a beauty of their own. It is so with
that old euphuism of the Elizabethan age—that pride of
dainty language and curious expression, which it is very
easy to ridicule, which often made itself ridiculous, but
which had below it a real sense of fitness and nicety;
and which, as we see in this very play, and still more
clearly in the sonnets, had some fascination for the young
Shakespeare himself. It is this foppery of delicate language, this fashionable plaything of his time, with which
Shakespeare is occupied in *Love's Labors Lost*. He shows
us the manner in all its stages, passing from the grotesque
and vulgar pedantry of Holofernes, through the extravagant but polished caricature of Armado, to become the
peculiar characteristic of a real though still quaint poetry
in Biron himself, who is still chargeable even at his best
with just a little affectation. As Shakespeare laughs
broadly at it in Holofernes or Armado, so he is the an-
alyst of its curious charm in Biron; and this analysis in-
volves a delicate raillery by Shakespeare himself at his
own chosen manner.

This "foppery" of Shakespeare's day had, then, its
really delightful side, a quality in no sense "affected,"
by which it satisfies a real instinct in our minds—the
fancy so many of us have for an exquisite and curious
skill in the use of words. Biron is the perfect flower of
this manner:

A man of fire-new words, fashion's own knight:

—as he describes Armado, in terms which are really

applicable to himself. In him this manner blends with a true gallantry of nature and an affectionate complaisance and grace. He has at times some of its extravagance or caricature also, but the shades of expression by which he passes from this to the "golden cadence" of Shakespeare's own most characteristic verse are so fine that it is sometimes difficult to trace them. What is a vulgarity in Holofernes, and a caricature in Armado, refines itself with him into the expression of a nature truly and inwardly bent upon a form of delicate perfection, and is accompanied by a real insight into the laws which determine what is exquisite in language and their root in the nature of things. He can appreciate quite the opposite style—

> In russet yeas, and honest kersey noes;

he knows the first law of pathos, that

> Honest plain words best suit the ear of grief.

He delights in his own rapidity of intuition; and, in harmony with the half-sensuous philosophy of the sonnets, exalts, a little scornfully, in many memorable expressions, the judgment of the senses, above all slower, more toilsome means of knowledge, scorning some who fail to see things only because they are so clear:

> So ere you find where light in darkness lies,
> Your light grows dark by losing of your eyes:—

as with some German commentators on Shakespeare. Appealing always to actual sensation from men's affected theories, he might seem to despise learning, as, indeed, he has taken up his deep studies partly in sport, and demands always the profit of learning in renewed enjoyment. Yet he surprises us from time to time by intuitions which could come only from a deep experience and power of observation; and men listen to him, old and young, in spite of themselves. He is quickly impressi-

ble to the slightest clouding of the spirits in social inter-
course, and has moments of extreme seriousness: his
trial-task may well be, as Rosaline puts it—

To enforce the pained impotent to smile.

But still, through all, he is true to his chosen manner:
that gloss of dainty language is a second nature with
him; even at his best he is not without a certain artifice;
the trick of playing on words never deserts him; and
Shakespeare, in whose own genius there is an element of
this very quality, shows us in this graceful, and, as it
seems, studied, portrait, his enjoyment of it.

As happens with every true dramatist, Shakespeare is
for the most part hidden behind the persons of his crea-
tion. Yet there are certain of his characters in which we
feel that there is something of self-portraiture. And it is
not so much in his grander, more subtle and ingenious
creations that we feel this—in *Hamlet* and *King Lear*—
as in those slighter and more spontaneously developed
figures, who, while far from playing principal parts, are
yet distinguished by a peculiar happiness and delicate
ease in the drawing of them—figures which possess,
above all, that winning attractiveness which there is no
man but would willingly exercise, and which resemble
those works of art which, though not meant to be very
great or imposing, are yet wrought of the choicest material. Mercutio, in *Romeo and Juliet*, belongs to this
group of Shakespeare's characters—versatile, mercurial
people, such as make good actors, and in whom the

Nimble spirits of the arteries,

the finer but still merely animal elements of great wit,
predominate. A careful delineation of minor, yet expres-
sive traits seems to mark them out as the characters of
his predilection; and it is hard not to identify him with
these more than with others. Biron, in *Love's Labors
Lost*, is perhaps the most striking member of this group.
In this character, which is never quite in touch, never

quite on a perfect level of understanding, with the other persons of the play, we see, perhaps, a reflex of Shakespeare himself, when he has just become able to stand aside from and estimate the first period of his poetry.

NORTHROP FRYE

The Argument of Comedy

The Greeks produced two kinds of comedy, Old Comedy, represented by the eleven extant plays of Aristophanes, and New Comedy, of which the best known
exponent is Menander. About two dozen New Comedies
survive in the work of Plautus and Terence. Old Comedy,
however, was out of date before Aristophanes himself
was dead; and today, when we speak of comedy, we normally think of something that derives from the Menandrine tradition.

New Comedy unfolds from what may be described as
a comic Oedipus situation. Its main theme is the successful effort of a young man to outwit an opponent and
possess the girl of his choice. The opponent is usually
the father (*senex*), and the psychological descent of the
heroine from the mother is also sometimes hinted at.
The father frequently wants the same girl, and is cheated
out of her by the son, the mother thus becoming the son's
ally. The girl is usually a slave or courtesan, and the plot
turns on a *cognitio* or discovery of birth which makes her
marriageable. Thus it turns out that she is not under an
insuperable taboo after all but is an accessible object of
desire, so that the plot follows the regular wish-fulfillment

From *English Institute Essays, 1948,* edited by D. A. Robertson. New
York: Columbia University Press, 1949. Copyright 1949 by Columbia
University Press. Reprinted by permission of the publisher.

pattern. Often the central Oedipus situation is thinly concealed by surrogates or doubles of the main characters, as when the heroine is discovered to be the hero's sister, and has to be married off to his best friend. In Congreve's *Love for Love,* to take a modern instance well within the Menandrine tradition, there are two Oedipus themes in counterpoint: the hero cheats his father out of the heroine, and his best friend violates the wife of an impotent old man who is the heroine's guardian. Whether this analysis is sound or not, New Comedy is certainly concerned with the maneuvering of a young man toward a young woman, and marriage is the tonic chord on which it ends. The normal comic resolution is the surrender of the *senex* to the hero, never the reverse. Shakespeare tried to reverse the pattern in *All's Well That Ends Well,* where the king of France forces Bertram to marry Helena, and the critics have not yet stopped making faces over it.

New Comedy has the blessing of Aristotle, who greatly preferred it to its predecessor, and it exhibits the general pattern of Aristotelian causation. It has a material cause in the young man's sexual desire, and a formal cause in the social order represented by the *senex,* with which the hero comes to terms when he gratifies his desire. It has an efficient cause in the character who brings about the final situation. In classical times this character is a tricky slave; Renaissance dramatists often use some adaptation of the medieval "vice"; modern writers generally like to pretend that nature, or at least the natural course of events, is the efficient cause. The final cause is the audience, which is expected by its applause to take part in the comic resolution. All this takes place on a single order of existence. The action of New Comedy tends to become probable rather than fantastic, and it moves toward realism and away from myth and romance. The one romantic (originally mythical) feature in it, the fact that the hero or heroine turns out to be freeborn or someone's heir, is precisely the feature that trained New Comedy audiences tire of most quickly.

The conventions of New Comedy are the conventions

of Jonson and Molière, and a fortiori of the English Restoration and the French rococo. When Ibsen started giving ironic twists to the same formulas, his startled hearers took them for portents of a social revolution. Even the old chestnut about the heroine's being really the hero's sister turns up in *Ghosts* and *Little Eyolf.* The average movie of today is a rigidly conventionalized New Comedy proceeding toward an act which, like death in Greek tragedy, takes place offstage, and is symbolized by the final embrace.

In all good New Comedy there is a social as well as an individual theme which must be sought in the general atmosphere of reconciliation that makes the final marriage possible. As the hero gets closer to the heroine and opposition is overcome, all the right-thinking people come over to his side. Thus a new social unit is formed on the stage, and the moment that this social unit crystallizes is the moment of the comic resolution. In the last scene, when the dramatist usually tries to get all his characters on the stage at once, the audience witnesses the birth of a renewed sense of social integration. In comedy as in life the regular expression of this is a festival, whether a marriage, a dance, or a feast. Old Comedy has, besides a marriage, a *komos,* the processional dance from which comedy derives its name; and the masque, which is a by-form of comedy, also ends in a dance.

This new social integration may be called, first, a kind of moral norm and, second, the pattern of a free society. We can see this more clearly if we look at the sort of characters who impede the progress of the comedy toward the hero's victory. These are always people who are in some kind of mental bondage, who are helplessly driven by ruling passions, neurotic compulsions, social rituals, and selfishness. The miser, the hypochondriac, the hypocrite, the pedant, the snob: these are humors, people who do not fully know what they are doing, who are slaves to a predictable self-imposed pattern of behavior. What we call the moral norm is, then, not morality but deliverance from moral bondage. Comedy is designed not to condemn evil, but to ridicule a lack of self-knowledge. It

THE ARGUMENT OF COMEDY

finds the virtues of Malvolio and Angelo as comic as the
vices of Shylock.

The essential comic resolution, therefore, is an individual release which is also a social reconciliation. The
normal individual is freed from the bonds of a humorous
society, and a normal society is freed from the bonds imposed on it by humorous individuals. The Oedipus pattern we noted in New Comedy belongs to the individual
side of this, and the sense of the ridiculousness of the
humor to the social side. But all real comedy is based on
the principle that these two forms of release are ultimately
the same: this principle may be seen at its most concentrated in *The Tempest*. The rule holds whether the
resolution is expressed in social terms, as in *The Merchant of Venice,* or in individual terms, as in Ibsen's *An
Enemy of the People.*

The freer the society, the greater the variety of individuals it can tolerate, and the natural tendency of comedy
is to include as many as possible in its final festival. The
motto of comedy is Terence's "Nothing human is alien to
me." This may be one reason for the traditional comic
importance of the parasite, who has no business to be at
the festival but is nevertheless there. The spirit of reconciliation which pervades the comedies of Shakespeare is
not to be ascribed to a personal attitude of his own, about
which we know nothing whatever, but to his impersonal
concentration on the laws of comic form.

Hence the moral quality of the society presented is not
the point of the comic resolution. In Jonson's *Volpone*
the final assertion of the moral norm takes the form of a
social revenge on Volpone, and the play ends with a great
bustle of sentences to penal servitude and the galleys. One
feels perhaps that the audience's sense of the moral norm
does not need so much hard labor. In *The Alchemist,*
when Lovewit returns to his house, the virtuous characters have proved so weak and the rascals so ingenious
that the action dissolves in laughter. Whichever is morally
the better ending, that of *The Alchemist* is more concentrated comedy. *Volpone* is starting to move toward

tragedy, toward the vision of a greatness which develops *hybris* and catastrophe.

The same principle is even clearer in Aristophanes. Aristophanes is the most personal of writers: his opinions on every subject are written all over his plays, and we have no doubt of his moral attitude. We know that he wanted peace with Sparta and that he hated Cleon, and when his comedy depicts the attaining of peace and the defeat of Cleon we know that he approved and wanted his audience to approve. But in *Ecclesiazusae* a band of women in disguise railroad a communistic scheme through the Assembly, which is a horrid parody of Plato's *Republic,* and proceed to inaugurate Plato's sexual communism with some astonishing improvements. Presumably Aristophanes did not applaud this, yet the comedy follows the same pattern and the same resolution. In *The Birds* the Peisthetairos who defies Zeus and blocks out Olympus with his Cloud-Cuckoo-Land is accorded the same triumph that is given to the Trygaeus of the *Peace* who flies to heaven and brings a golden age back to Athens.

Comedy, then, may show virtue her own feature and scorn her own image—for Hamlet's famous definition of drama was originally a definition of comedy. It may emphasize the birth of an ideal society as you like it, or the tawdriness of the sham society which is the way of the world. There is an important parallel here with tragedy. Tragedy, we are told, is expected to raise but not ultimately to accept the emotions of pity and terror. These I take to be the sense of moral good and evil, respectively, which we attach to the tragic hero. He may be as good as Caesar, and so appeal to our pity, or as bad as Macbeth, and so appeal to terror, but the particular thing called tragedy that happens to him does not depend on his moral status. The tragic catharsis passes beyond moral judgment, and while it is quite possible to construct a moral tragedy, what tragedy gains in morality it loses in cathartic power. The same is true of the comic catharsis, which raises sympathy and ridicule on a moral basis, but passes beyond both.

Many things are involved in the tragic catharsis, but one of them is a mental or imaginative form of the sacrificial ritual out of which tragedy arose. This is the ritual of the struggle, death, and rebirth of a God-Man, which is linked to the yearly triumph of spring over winter. The tragic hero is not really killed, and the audience no longer eats his body and drinks his blood, but the corresponding thing in art still takes place. The audience enters into communion with the body of the hero, becoming thereby a single body itself. Comedy grows out of the same ritual, for in the ritual the tragic story has a comic sequel. Divine men do not die: they die and rise again. The ritual pattern behind the catharsis of comedy is the resurrection that follows the death, the epiphany or manifestation of the risen hero. This is clear enough in Aristophanes, where the hero is treated as a risen God-Man, led in triumph with the divine honors of the Olympic victor, rejuvenated, or hailed as a new Zeus. In New Comedy the new human body is, as we have seen, both a hero and a social group. Aristophanes is not only closer to the ritual pattern, but contemporary with Plato; and his comedy, unlike Menander's, is Platonic and dialectic: it seeks not the entelechy of the soul but the Form of the Good, and finds it in the resurrection of the soul from the world of the cave to the sunlight. The audience gains a vision of that resurrection whether the conclusion is joyful or ironic, just as in tragedy it gains a vision of a heroic death whether the hero is morally innocent or guilty.

Two things follow from this: first, that tragedy is really implicit or uncompleted comedy; second, that comedy contains a potential tragedy within itself. With regard to the latter, Aristophanes is full of traces of the original death of the hero which preceded his resurrection in the ritual. Even in New Comedy the dramatist usually tries to bring his action as close to a tragic overthrow of the hero as he can get it, and reverses this movement as suddenly as possible. In Plautus the tricky slave is often forgiven or even freed after having been threatened with all the brutalities that a very brutal dramatist can think of, including crucifixion. Thus the resolution of New Comedy

seems to be a realistic foreshortening of a death-and-res-
urrection pattern, in which the struggle and rebirth of a
divine hero has shrunk into a marriage, the freeing of a
slave, and the triumph of a young man over an older one.

As for the conception of tragedy as implicit comedy,
we may notice how often tragedy closes on the major
chord of comedy: the Aeschylean trilogy, for instance,
proceeds to what is really a comic resolution, and so do
many tragedies of Euripides. From the point of view of
Christianity, too, tragedy is an episode in that larger
scheme of redemption and resurrection to which Dante
gave the name of *commedia*. This conception of *commedia*
enters drama with the miracle-play cycles, where such
tragedies as the Fall and the Crucifixion are episodes of a
dramatic scheme in which the divine comedy has the last
word. The sense of tragedy as a prelude to comedy is
hardly separable from anything explicitly Christian. The
serenity of the final double chorus in the St. Matthew
Passion would hardly be attainable if composer and audience did not know that there was more to the story. Nor
would the death of Samson lead to "calm of mind all
passion spent" if Samson were not a prototype of the
rising Christ.

New Comedy is thus contained, so to speak, within the
symbolic structure of Old Comedy, which in its turn is
contained within the Christian conception of *commedia*.
This sounds like a logically exhaustive classification, but
we have still not caught Shakespeare in it.

It is only in Jonson and the Restoration writers that
English comedy can be called a form of New Comedy.
The earlier tradition established by Peele and developed
by Lyly, Greene, and the masque writers, which uses
themes from romance and folklore and avoids the comedy
of manners, is the one followed by Shakespeare. These
themes are largely medieval in origin, and derive, not
from the mysteries or the moralities or the interludes,
but from a fourth dramatic tradition. This is the drama
of folk ritual, of the St. George play and the mummers'
play, of the feast of the ass and the Boy Bishop, and of
all the dramatic activity that punctuated the Christian

calendar with the rituals of an immemorial paganism. We may call this the drama of the green world, and its theme is once again the triumph of life over the waste land, the death and revival of the year impersonated by figures still human, and once divine as well.

When Shakespeare began to study Plautus and Terence, his dramatic instinct, stimulated by his predecessors, divined that there was a profounder pattern in the argument of comedy than appears in either of them. At once—for the process is beginning in *The Comedy of Errors*—he started groping toward that profounder pattern, the ritual of death and revival that also underlies Aristophanes, of which an exact equivalent lay ready to hand in the drama of the green world. This parallelism largely accounts for the resemblances to Greek ritual which Colin Still has pointed out in *The Tempest*.

The Two Gentlemen of Verona is an orthodox New Comedy except for one thing. The hero Valentine becomes captain of a band of outlaws in a forest, and all the other characters are gathered into this forest and become converted. Thus the action of the comedy begins in a world represented as a normal world, moves into the green world, goes into a metamorphosis there in which the comic resolution is achieved, and returns to the normal world. The forest in this play is the embryonic form of the fairy world of *A Midsummer Night's Dream,* the Forest of Arden in *As You Like It,* Windsor Forest in *The Merry Wives of Windsor,* and the pastoral world of the mythical sea-coasted Bohemia in *The Winter's Tale.* In all these comedies there is the same rhythmic movement from normal world to green world and back again. Nor is this second world confined to the forest comedies. In *The Merchant of Venice* the two worlds are a little harder to see, yet Venice is clearly not the same world as that of Portia's mysterious house in Belmont, where there are caskets teaching that gold and silver are corruptible goods, and from whence proceed the wonderful cosmological harmonies of the fifth act. In *The Tempest* the entire action takes place in the second world, and the same may be said of *Twelfth Night,* which, as its title implies, presents a carnival society, not so much a green world as an ever-green one. The second world is absent from the so-called problem comedies, which is one of the things that makes them problem comedies.

The green world charges the comedies with a symbol-ism in which the comic resolution contains a suggestion of the old ritual pattern of the victory of summer over winter. This is explicit in *Love's Labor's Lost*. In this very masque-like play, the comic contest takes the form of the medieval debate of winter and spring. In *The Merry Wives of Windsor* there is an elaborate ritual of the defeat of winter, known to folklorists as "carrying out Death," of which Falstaff is the victim; and Falstaff must have felt that, after being thrown into the water, dressed up as a witch and beaten out of a house with curses, and finally supplied with a beast's head and singed with candles while he said, "Divide me like a brib'd buck, each a haunch," he had done about all that could reasonably be asked of any fertility spirit.

The association of this symbolism with the death and revival of human beings is more elusive, but still percep-tible. The fact that the heroine often brings about the comic resolution by disguising herself as a boy is familiar enough. In the Hero of *Much Ado About Nothing* and the Helena of *All's Well That Ends Well*, this theme of the withdrawal and return of the heroine comes as close to a death and revival as Elizabethan conventions will allow. The Thaisa of *Pericles* and the Fidele of *Cymbeline* are beginning to crack the conventions, and with the disap-pearance and revival of Hermione in *The Winter's Tale*, who actually returns once as a ghost in a dream, the orig-inal nature-myth of Demeter and Proserpine is openly established. The fact that the dying and reviving character is usually female strengthens the feeling that there is something maternal about the green world, in which the new order of the comic resolution is nourished and brought to birth. However, a similar theme which is very like the rejuvenation of the *senex* so frequent in Aristophanes occurs in the folklore motif of the healing of the impotent king on which *All's Well That Ends Well* is based, and this theme is probably involved in the symbolism of Prospero.

The conception of a second world bursts the boundaries of Menandrine comedy, yet it is clear that the world of Puck is no world of eternal forms or divine revelation. Shakespeare's comedy is not Aristotelian and realistic like Menander's, nor Platonic and dialectic like Aristophanes', nor Thomist and sacramental like Dante's, but a fourth kind. It is an Elizabethan kind, and is not confined either to Shakespeare or to the drama. Spenser's epic is a wonderful contrapuntal intermingling of two orders of existence, one the red and white world of English history, the other the green world of the Faerie Queene. The latter is a world of crusading virtues proceeding from the Faerie Queene's court and designed to return to that court when the destiny of the other world is fulfilled. The fact that the Faerie Queene's knights are sent out during the twelve days of the Christmas festival suggests our next point.

Shakespeare too has his green world of comedy and his red and white world of history. The story of the latter is at one point interrupted by an invasion from the comic world, when Falstaff *senex et parasitus* throws his gigantic shadow over Prince Henry, assuming on one occasion the role of his father. Clearly, if the Prince is ever to conquer France he must reassert the moral norm. The moral norm is duly reasserted, but the rejection of Falstaff is not a comic resolution. In comedy the moral norm is not morality but deliverance, and we certainly do not feel delivered from Falstaff as we feel delivered from Shylock with his absurd and vicious bond. The moral norm does not carry with it the vision of a free society: Falstaff will always keep a bit of that in his tavern.

Falstaff is a mock king, a lord of misrule, and his tavern is a Saturnalia. Yet we are reminded of the original meaning of the Saturnalia, as a rite intended to recall the golden age of Saturn. Falstaff's world is not a golden world, but as long as we remember it we cannot forget that the world of *Henry V* is an iron one. We are reminded too of another traditional denizen of the green world, Robin Hood, the outlaw who manages to suggest a better kind of society than those who make him an out-law can produce. The outlaws in *The Two Gentlemen of Verona* compare themselves, in spite of the Italian set-ting, to Robin Hood, and in *As You Like It* Charles the wrestler says of Duke Senior's followers: "There they live like the old Robin Hood of England: they say many young gentlemen flock to him every day, and fleet the time carelessly, as they did in the golden world."

In the histories, therefore, the comic Saturnalia is a temporary reversal of normal standards, comic "relief" as it is called, which subsides and allows the history to continue. In the comedies, the green world suggests an original golden age which the normal world has usurped and which makes us wonder if it is not the normal world that is the real Saturnalia. In *Cymbeline* the green world finally triumphs over a historical theme, the reason being perhaps that in that play the incarnation of Christ, which is contemporary with Cymbeline, takes place offstage, and accounts for the halcyon peace with which the play concludes. From then on in Shakespeare's plays, the green world has it all its own way, and both in *Cymbeline* and in *Henry VIII* there may be suggestions that Shake-speare, like Spenser, is moving toward a synthesis of the two worlds, a wedding of Prince Arthur and the Faerie Queene.

This world of fairies, dreams, disembodied souls, and pastoral lovers may not be a "real" world, but, if not, there is something equally illusory in the stumbling and blinded follies of the "normal" world, of Theseus' Athens with its idiotic marriage law, of Duke Frederick and his melancholy tyranny, of Leontes and his mad jealousy, of the Court Party with their plots and intrigues. The famous speech of Prospero about the dream nature of reality applies equally to Milan and the enchanted island. We spend our lives partly in a waking world we call normal and partly in a dream world which we create out of our own desires. Shakespeare endows both worlds with equal imaginative power, brings them opposite one another, and makes each world seem unreal when seen by the light of the other. He uses freely both the heroic triumph of

New Comedy and the ritual resurrection of its predecessor, but his distinctive comic resolution is different from either: it is a detachment of the spirit born of this reciprocal reflection of two illusory realities. We need not ask whether this brings us into a higher order of existence or not, for the question of existence is not relevant to poetry.

We have spoken of New Comedy as Aristotelian, Old Comedy as Platonic and Dante's *commedia* as Thomist, but it is difficult to suggest a philosophical spokesman for the form of Shakespeare's comedy. For Shakespeare, the subject matter of poetry is not life, or nature, or reality, or revelation, or anything else that the philosopher builds on, but poetry itself, a verbal universe. That is one reason why he is both the most elusive and the most substantial of poets.

RICHARD DAVID

from *Shakespeare's Comedies and the Modern Stage*

[A study of production problems with particular reference to *Love's Labor's Lost* at the New Theatre (1949–50) . . .]

Dr. Johnson was the last critic who dared to say that Shakespeare's most characteristic and most inspired work lay in his comedies. The Romantics, putting an exaggerated value on tragedy as in some way nearer to the heart of the matter, degraded the comedies to the status of potboilers; and even today we have hardly escaped from the Romantics' spell. We have one expounder of the comedies for every ten on the tragedies; and for a Granville-Barker to stoop to *A Midsummer Night's Dream,* or an Edith Evans to Rosalind, is exceptional.

We may not agree with Johnson that the comedies deserve more effort than the tragedies, but clearly they require more if they are to make a comparable impression on a modern audience. Tragedy is large in gesture and

From *Shakespeare Survey 4* (1951), edited by Allardyce Nicoll, 129–35. Reprinted by permission of Richard David and the Cambridge University Press.

effect, and even when its overtones are lost and the subsidiary strokes bungled, its main import can hardly be
missed. Comedy depends much more on detail, on delicate adjustments of balance and of contrast; it seeks to
reproduce the climate rather than the actual predicaments
of real life and its method is rather allusiveness than direct presentation. Comedy has more and finer points of
attachment to the world in which it is composed than
has tragedy. For this reason, comedy dates the more rap-
idly and the more thoroughly, and after a lapse of years
a tragedy based even on so fantastic a convention as
Fletcher's is easier to grasp than a comedy of Jonson or
Middleton, for all its firm grounding in human nature.
Tragedy can be understood in the original, as it were,
even by those unacquainted with the tongue; whereas
comedy, to be appreciated by a modern audience, must
undergo some degree of translation into modern terms.

The difficulties that face the would-be translator are
broadly of two kinds. Some old comedies have remained
crystal clear in intention, though the details of the action
and of the language through which that intention is con-
veyed are now largely incomprehensible without a gloss;
in others, language and action are perfectly plain and yet
the point of the whole has become obscure or capable of
various interpretations. These peculiar difficulties are well
exemplified in two distinguished recent productions, the
Love's Labor's Lost directed by Hugh Hunt for the Old
Vic Company in the winter of 1949–50, and Peter
Brook's *Measure for Measure,* with which the Stratford
Memorial Theatre opened its 1950 season. Whatever may
be the topical implications of *Love's Labor's Lost* its
main point is plain—the gentle ragging of youthful prig-
gishness and affectation, as measured against natural good
sense and natural good feeling—and it is a point that
time has not dulled. Dons and donnishness are today
even more popular as butts than they were in the 1590's,
and the vivacity controlled by a good heart that Shakespeare praises is a virtue that does not grow stale. On
the other hand, the almost Joycean reduplication of puns
and the obscure allusions of the play are a byword. *Meas-*

ure for Measure is by comparison straightforwardness itself as far as the text goes; but the arguments as to whether the piece is comedy or problem-play, Isabella heroine or caricature, are unending.

Even though the intention of *Love's Labor's Lost* may be plain enough, some skill is required in the presentation to convey it to a modern audience. The point or moral of the play (as of so many comedies) is a code of manners, a demonstration of what rational behavior should be by a comparison with irrational behavior. Nathaniel is unwittingly providing an ironic commentary on himself and his peers when he says of Dull:

> . . . such barren plants are set before us, that we thankful
>   should be,
> Which we of taste and feeling are, for those parts that do
>   fructify in us more than he.
>
> (IV.ii.29–30)

The standards set are those of taste and feeling, aristocratic standards, and the ladies must live up to them—the lords, too, once they have come to their senses. Moreover, the audience must be conscious throughout that the action is enclosed in a coherent and self-contained world defined by these standards.

The coherence of the play was admirably preserved in the Old Vic production. The sets perfectly suggested the self-contained world of Navarre's park, shut away among steep hillslopes down which the hanging woods cascaded, excluding the everyday world and blanketing every sound that might penetrate from it. Among the trees showed the turrets of castles and hunting lodges, each retreat and secret corner of the domain isolated from the others by the waters of a spreading lake that was at the same time the means of communication between them. One may criticize the elaboration and heaviness of this set. It was no doubt suggested by the backgrounds to Elizabethan miniatures, the more extended works of Hillyard or of Oliver; but enlarged to backcloth scale the effect was baroque rather than renaissance, more

Jacobean than Elizabethan. It accorded well with the autumnal ending of the play, but hardly with the green goose season of its opening. The devotees are solemn enough, but their solemnity must be seen to be against nature; the landscape (if we must have one) should be a laughing landscape that mocks their sober suits and matches the frills and freshness of the ladies through whose eyes we judge them. And yet the sense of a private and self-sufficient world, so successfully achieved in this production, owed much to the swathing and insistent scenery.

The structure of the play is uncomplicated. The first three acts present the situation and the opposing parties in bold and simple colors. Act IV is a helter-skelter with everyone at cross purposes, diversified by the to and fro of the hunt and the entrances of the comics. The long last scene builds up slowly but steadily, becoming more and more fantastic and ebullient until the appearance of Marcade bursts the bubble in an instant; this is one of the greatest *coups de théâtre* in Shakespeare, and it brings, after the whirlwind of fooling that has preceded it, the still small voice of sincerity and actuality before the play dissolves in thin air and birdsong. Hugh Hunt divided the whole naturally enough into three movements, each set in a different part of the labyrinthine park. In the first the nobles of Navarre made their pact to forego female company, and rated Costard the clown for his transgression of it; at the same spot Armado wandered ashore, from a boat paddled by Moth, to meet the disquieting vision of Jaquenetta; here too the ladies of the French embassy, advancing through the forest glades, were intercepted by Navarre and his courtiers. The focus of the second movement was a rustic cottage, again by the waterside, which provided shelter for Armado's lovesick meditations, and a prison for Costard; after the hunt arranged for the entertainment of the French ladies had swept by, it served as a convenient hiding place from which the eavesdropping lords could overhear each other's confession of forbidden love, and a rendezvous for Armado and the other devisers of his pageant. The last

movement (that is, the last scene of the play) opened
with the ladies idling outside their pavilion; to them the
masques of the Russians and of the Nine Worthies; and
over the lake at their back, when the merriment was at
its height, loomed the barge that brings the funereal Marcade with his news of the French King's death to cloud
the scene. The management of this effect was overwhelm-
ingly successful, as was the quiet recapitulation of the
lovers' problems that follows, and the final fading of the
play in trills and falling darkness. This by itself was full
justification for both setting and production.

Such elaborate dressing and marshaling of the action,
though foreign to Shakespeare's theater, is legitimate as
the just translation of his intention into modern terms.
The original audience of a coterie play or a play of manners (and *Love's Labor's Lost* is in some sense this)
is specially conditioned, by the community of interests
it shares with the author, to appreciate the mood of his
work and accept his illusion. A modern audience, unused
even to the unifying and sharpening effect of verse, may
well be encouraged to draw the same sense of characteristic atmosphere from scenery and direction. In some of
his efforts to this end Hunt nevertheless went outside his
brief.

The play must open with a tableau of the lords sign-
ing their solemn declaration. It is tidy and elegant to
balance this, at the point where the ladies are to take
over the lead, with a similar tableau of the feminine
party, and the last movement in the Old Vic production
accordingly opened with a "still" of the ladies outside
their pavilion. Shakespeare, however, has made no al-
lowance for this, nor has he provided accompanying action. What are the ladies to do? They shall sing a song
in chorus. This is "pretty and apt," but something ir-
relevant has been added to Shakespeare.

There were other instances of this striving to impose
an extra formality on an already formal play. The second
movement was rounded off—after Armado and Holofernes had completed their plans for the pageant—with
a burlesque dance in which *all* the comics joined. Now it

may be appropriate, as Granville-Barker has suggested, that Dull should here dance a few steps of his hay to show what he thinks is a suitable entertainment for the gentlefolk; but for Armado or Holofernes, who has just expressed his disgust at Dull's low suggestion, to take part in it is to deny their nature, and at this point of the play they must still be true to themselves. At the end, when comedy slips imperceptibly into vaudeville, let them dance their jig if you will. A more blatant, though less serious, reversal of Shakespeare's intention for the sake of spectacle occurred in the last movement, when the Russian maskers are begging the ladies for a dance. "Play music then," says the mock princess. "Nay, you must do it soon. Not yet? No dance. Thus change I like the moon." In the Old Vic production a formal dance did in fact follow the words "Play music then," and continued some time before Rosaline, resuming her broken speech, brought the measure to an end. Yet it is clear that the lords, though constantly tantalized into thinking that the ladies may dance with them, are as constantly put off. Ten lines later the King is still begging the "princess" to begin.

Such dislocations, the first of dramatic propriety, the second of literal meaning, could hardly be justified even if the added dances succeeded perfectly in reinforcing the tone or continuity of the action. Here they had the opposite effect. The movements were perfunctory, the music feeble and banal to a degree. Yet even perfectly designed music and choreography would here have been an intrusion, a formal element introduced just where the text avoids it. Shakespeare has given plenty of opportunities in this play for formality, and we have now to see the opposite error, of trying to break down a given artificiality and make the scenes of spectacle "come to life." The tableaux, or scenes of ceremony, demand some supporting cast, and no doubt Shakespeare gave his king and princess as large a train of attendants as his company could muster. The sole function of these extras, however, is to add weight and volume to the dignity of their masters, and any attempt to give depth to the scene by making indi-

viduals of them is totally un-Shakespearian. A tendency
to "work up" the crowd is one of the most dangerous
features of modern productions of Shakespeare. In *Love's
Labor's Lost,* it is true, there was nothing to equal the
horrors of Komisarjevsky's *King Lear,* in which the hundred knights, vociferously echoing their master's "Return
with her?," effectively broke not only the rhythm but the
mounting tension of one of Shakespeare's greatest dramatic crescendos. The interpolations which the ladies
were allowed to make in Boyet's reading of Armado's
love letter were exactly similar but in this context harm-
less; while the caperings and posturings and beard-wag-
gings of the burlesque philosophers in Navarre's train,
which were employed to "lighten" the King's first speech
and his reception of the ladies' embassy, were not so much
destroying Shakespeare's intention, as grossly overplaying
it. The solemn performance of Navarre and his peers has
indeed its anti-masque; but that is later provided by
Armado, Holofernes and Nathaniel and no duplication
of it is needed. It was again an overzealous striving for
vigor and variety that made a pantomime of the hunting
scene.

Finally, a rather different form of overemphasis. At
the beginning of the last scene the ladies' lighthearted
chatter about Cupid suddenly steadies as Rosaline says
to Katharine:

> You'll ne'er be friends with him, 'a killed your sister.

Katharine's reply introduces the first note of seriousness
into the play:

> He made her melancholy, sad, and heavy—
> And so she died: had she been light, like you,
> Of such a merry, nimble, stirring spirit,
> She might ha' been a grandam ere she died.

Hunt properly seized on this as a forecast of the serious
mood of the end of the play. For a moment the sun is
hidden by a forerunner of those clouds that are later to

overcast the scene, and we get a premonition of love's labor *lost*. This is admirable; but the mood was unduly prolonged in the repartee that follows between the two girls, which was worked up into a real quarrel, so that the Princess' "I beshrew all shrows" had to be delivered *tutta forza* in order to quell it. This gave a change of tempo and color, and showed us a new side of Rosaline's character, a hard shrewish side; but at this stage of the play neither the action nor the character has been sufficiently developed to bear this elaboration, and the only result was to turn the audience against so viperish a heroine.

This prolonged analysis of faults has been undertaken to show how the producer with the very best intentions —of giving continuity or variety to his play—may achieve the exact opposite. In general, however, the total mood of the play—buoyant, lyrical, penetrating, extravagant— had been so firmly and truly established by both producer and actors that it could not be shattered by incidental "wrong notes." As Elizabethans and as courtiers the ladies were perhaps more convincing than the men, who had a touch of the hobbledehoy about them; but that did little harm in a play wherein the ladies must show a superiority of wit and grace throughout, for all that their task is the harder, since there is less of substance in their badinage and only an exactly calculated bravura of speech and movement can carry it off. The greater delicacy of the ladies' playing was, however, counterbalanced by Michael Redgrave's performance as Berowne. He succeeded not only in conveying the wit, the wisdom and the vitality of the man, but in making him completely sympathetic to the audience. The great set speech of act IV, Scene i—"And I forsooth in love," in which he takes the audience into his confidence, was a *tour de force*. The speech is by no means easy, for many of its terms and turns of expression are obsolete today; but by treating it simply and directly, by trusting himself to the words (and his confidence clearly grew with practice), he made its point clear and its effect captivating.

The comic performances in no way betrayed the stand-

ard set by those of the straight parts, although (as, alas,
so often happens) their unnecessary business seemed to
increase and to get more out of hand as the run of the
play proceeded. George Benson gave us the perfect Costard; would that all players of Shakepearian clowns were
as direct and bold and true to the text as this. On the
other hand, the Holofernes and the Nathaniel were rather
translations into modern equivalents—a Will Hay or a
Groucho Marx with his stooge. This is legitimate; the
Crazy Gang or the Itma comics are today the closest in
line of descent to the figures of the Commedia dell'arte
from whom the fantastics of *Love's Labor's Lost* derive.
The only characters that were totally off key were Armado
and Moth, presented as a seedy Don Quixote and a
ragged urchin. Now it is of the essence of both figures
that they are of the Court (Dull and Costard are quite
enough to represent the bumpkins). Armado is as much
an exquisite as Osric. It is part of the joke that his finery
is only on the surface (he cannot afford a shirt) but his
every effort goes into maintaining the *appearance* of
finery, and finery it is. Moth is the cheeky page boy, a
"cit" if ever there was one, and a diminutive echo of his
master's finicking fashion. The humor of their inter-
changes, already precarious after the lapse of three and
a half centuries, fades utterly if they are presented not
as the lightning duels of court rapiers but as the rustic's
solemn game of quarterstaff.

This brings us to the consideration of the topical jokes
and private humors that make up so large a part of the
dialogue, particularly between the farcical characters, and
present the second and more troublesome problem to
any would-be translator for the modern stage. There
would seem to be four ways of dealing with this largely
deadwood: (1) to cut the passage altogether; (2) to accompany it with some entirely extraneous piece of business, in the hope that this will distract attention from
the words, which are "thrown away" as best may be; (3)
to have the words spoken against music which will render
them inaudible; (4) to try the passage straight and hope
that *someone* will see, or pretend to see, the joke—at least

the purists will be satisfied. The purists of course will object strongly to the first solution, but I do not see how with some passages it can be avoided if the performance of the play is to be living entertainment and not merely a (possibly edifying) ritual. Solutions two and three are clearly abominable, and though one would like always to see the direct method given a trial there are some things it cannot save. The trouble is that producers will differ in their judgment of what can be saved and what must be cut, and most of them are likely to err on the side of pessimism.

The Old Vic production used all four methods. Of the seven cruces that have notoriously baffled or divided commentators only two, the "envoy" of the fox, the ape and the humble-bee, and the play of Holofernes and Moth on "piercing a hogshead," were cut (and rightly cut) *in toto*. The "tender juvenal," the "school of night," and the "charge-house on the mountain" were all given their chance, perhaps in the belief that their ill fame was too great for them to be ignored. Armado's odd salutation —"Chirrah"—was also left in, together with the reference to an eel that so strangely annoys him on his first appearance. This proved a dangerous course, however, at least in the case of the eel, for with the disappearance of the real occasion of the joke it was necessary to drop Armado's inexplicable irritation at it ("Thou heat'st my blood") and invent a new cue for it. Moth therefore made his entrance carrying a real eel, which he might be supposed recently to have fished out of the encircling lake; and I suspect this detail conditioned the producer's whole view of Moth's (and, with him, Armado's) appearance and status, which I have already tried to show were misconceived.

Some other jokes, of which the point is known but cannot be explained without a considerable gloss, were also wisely cut: Moth's play with the four complexions, his skirmish with Holofernes over sheep and vowels, and most of the "greasy" talk between Boyet and Maria at the end of the hunting scene. There was little excuse, however, for devoting to the same extinction such simple puns as those on style, stile and climbing in the merriness, or the frequent and pertinent comments on the fantastics' inability to count; and it was surely strange, if these were to go, that such obvious interpolations as the duplicated versions of the lovers' first dialogues, and Costard's comments on a vanished entry for Armado and Moth in the hunting scene, should have been spared to puzzle us.

Of the second method of dealing with an obscure passage, the introduction of distracting business, there were three prominent examples, two of them particularly unhappy. It was perhaps allowable that Dull, in the midst of Nathaniel's wordy tirade on his insensitivity, should be discovered to be carrying, apparently without being aware of it or discommoded by it, an arrow from the hunt still firmly embedded in his posterior. This is at least a fair gloss on Nathaniel's "only sensible in the duller parts"; but the disproportionate laughter it aroused in the audience shattered the continuity of the scene and the delicate balance between its actors. The other two instances of this technique were unhappy because the jokes so painstakingly masked remain perfectly valid ones today and if allowed to make their own effect would have raised greater and more relevant amusement than their substitutes. When Jaquenetta brings Berowne's letter to Nathaniel to interpret, Holofernes is consumed with curiosity to see it but feels it would be beneath his dignity to look over the Curate's shoulder. He therefore pretends to be very much absorbed in his own thoughts, on a plane far above mere mundane affairs. He murmurs (incorrectly) a verse from Mantuan, hums the notes of the scale (again wrongly) all the time striving, under cover of this pretended abstraction, to get a glimpse of the letter. In the Old Vic production all this was thrown away to the accompaniment of a stupid piece of byplay in which Nathaniel tried surreptitiously to put his arm round the trusting Jaquenetta and found himself embracing Costard instead. This is entirely out of character for the Curate, while the Pedant's itch to meddle, sacrificed for it, is a typical and essential trait. Again, when the comics return from the dinner to which Holofernes has invited Nathaniel to witness his eloquence, the Curate is more than ever impressed by his host's superior learning. When Holofernes utters a particularly choice word Nathaniel, according to a direction in the original First Quarto text, draws out his notebook and with admiring comments records the *trouvaille*. In place of this characteristic and revealing action, Hunt made his players enter as if tipsy, and for the unction and the notebook of the toady substituted slurred syllables and some sorry business with a bottle. This is presumption.

To resort to the third way out, on the other hand, is the rankest cowardice, and it speaks well for the Old Vic production that this all too popular device was only used once, for the admittedly involved and paradoxical lines in which Boyet describes to the ladies how, Navarre having fallen in love at first sight, all his faculties are concentrated in his longing gaze. This speech was half chanted to a musical accompaniment to which Boyet's audience swayed in time. The effect was odious, but it was certainly impossible that many words should be caught, much less interpreted. It was perhaps surprising that the producer should have funked this passage when such teasers as "Light seeking light doth light of light beguile," and many of the "sets of wit," were left to take care of themselves, and did so very nicely.

JOHN ARTHOS

Love's Labor's Lost on the Stage

Love's Labor's Lost was written about 1595, but the first printing, in quarto, is dated 1598: "A Pleasant Conceited Comedie Called, Loues labors lost. As it was presented before her Highnes this last Christmas. Newly corrected and augmented By W. Shakespere."

A certain irony attaches to the next production of the play, which was offered as part of the Christmas festivities of 1604. The Earl of Southampton, having been imprisoned for his part in the plot of Essex against Queen Elizabeth, in celebrating his release by King James entertained the King and Queen at his house with a production of the play. There was an agreeable humor in choosing a play in which the chief male persons, men of royal and noble rank, propose to abandon life in the great world in order to pursue a celibate existence in an academy, a theme not wholly incongruous under the circumstances. The humor would have been apparent to the King, and what is topical in the play—in particular references to relations between England and France—also would have suggested matters of interest to the King.

The second quarto (1631) tells that the play was publicly acted at the Black-Friars and the Globe, but no record of these productions is known to survive. There is no mention of a performance of the play in Henslowe's and Pepys's diaries, and Genest, who surveyed all productions of Shakespeare's plays from 1642 till 1830, found no notice of *Love's Labor's Lost* in all that time.

Explanations for the neglect of the work center upon the opinion that the wordplay was so pervasive and complex that it was not stageworthy. There was also the frequent judgment that the supposed topicality was obscure and distracting. The critical reservations expressed by Hazlitt and Coleridge may also have been influential.

Madame Vestris, however, a gifted and popular actress, saw in the play the opportunity to make the most of the women's parts and put it on in the new Olympic theatre in London in 1839. Although it was praised, it held the stage for only a few days, despite what was said to have been a talented cast.

The next notices available are of productions at Sadler's Wells in 1857 and, surprisingly, at the Arch Street Theater in Philadelphia in 1858. And it was in the United States, at Augustin Daly's theater in New York—in 1873 and again in 1891—that the marvelous quality of the work was evidently understood and appreciated. The liberties Daly took with the text were considerable, yet one may judge from the prefatory remarks attached to the prompter's copy that they were as thoughtfully conceived as they were successful. For example: "The pageant is transposed to the end of the comedy, which closes with one of the sweetest of all the Shakespeare melodies and leaves its spectators with a mental vision of all the lovely spring flowers that grow on Avon's banks." *The New York Herald*'s critic was most enthusiastic:

> The skill with which the sense of atmosphere and expanse was given to the forest scenes was delightful. The tableau of winter showed an ice-hung scene, in the midst of which a snow-clad figure sang the strongly picturesque lines beginning 'When icicles hang'. Spring was indicated by a Watteau tableau of great brilliancy. Cunning shepherds and shepherdesses sat on mossy elevations, fountains gurgled, arbors twined, gloomily green vistas

opened, dazzling flowers and foliage spread seeming
fragrance and rich growth, and over all fell a shower of
changing light. The acting was respectable throughout,
with special excellence in the case of Miss Dyas, whose
refinement, intelligence and vivacity exhausted all the
significance contained in the role of the Princess. . . .
The costumes were brilliant beyond all precedent and
description. From beginning to end, the comedy was
placed upon the stage in the most generous and splendid
style.

With such a success one might have believed the play
would be entering upon a new life in the theater, but there
was to be, in fact, another long dry spell before *Love's
Labor's Lost* was to establish its appeal securely, and we
may only conclude that the times were not yet ripe for it
despite this remarkable example.

There is no record of another production before the
one at the Old Vic in 1906 and another at Stratford in
1907. There were three productions at the Old Vic in the
next thirty years, but Tyrone Guthrie's in 1936 was accounted a failure even with Edith Evans as Rosaline and
Michael Redgrave as the King of Navarre. There were a
few successes at the Open Air Theatre in Regent's Park.
It was only in 1946 that Peter Brook's "landmark" production demonstrated such attractive qualities in the work
that it is credited with leading the way for the more than
ninety productions in the English-speaking world in the
next three decades.

Brook had seen a production in French at the Odéon in
Paris in 1945 in which the pictorial potentialities of the
play were effectively developed. J. Dapoigny had devised
settings and provided costumes with the paintings of
Watteau in mind: "The style of Watteau's dresses with its
broad undecorated expanses of billowing satin seemed the
ideal visual correlative of the essential sweet-sad mood of
the play." (It is a curious coincidence that Daly's production had brought Watteau to the mind of the New York
critic.)

Still, more than a pictorial emphasis was involved,

however, in the stimulus Brook took from this production. The theories and practices of Artaud and Genet were also involved in the French adaptation, and Brook was evidently inspired by the rejection of naturalism and in particular by the refusal to be bound by the constraints imposed when adhering to normal time patterns. To begin with, this meant to Brook that a Shakespeare play should not be offered as a period piece; it should be wholly free of antiquarian appeal. He has made the point this way, in *The Empty Space*: "I dressed the character called the Constable Dull as a Victorian policeman because his name conjured up the typical figure of the London bobby. For other reasons the rest of the characters were dressed in Watteau-eighteenth-century clothes, but no one was conscious of an anachronism." He put the case in this way: the aim of drama is toward "immediacy." "A representation is the occasion when something is represented that once was, now is. For representation is not an imitation or a description of a past event, a representation denies time. It abolishes the difference between yesterday and today."

The success of Brook's production of *Love's Labor's Lost* was thus in part the success of the new drama, leading the way to other productions of the play that were to be equally free of the constraints of naturalistic imitation and as open to transformation. The example was evidently so attractive that in the years following it was a rare undertaking, such as the reputedly exquisite staging of Hugh Hunt's in 1949 at the New Theater, that aimed to capture the atmosphere of an Elizabethan production, although here, too, the pictorial emphasis Brook had made so much of was key to the success of this production, Hunt following Nicholas Hillyard rather than Watteau. He also stressed the lyrical potentialities of the work, even in the humorous exchanges, and with such emphasis on choreography as to recall the manner of masques. Hunt was profoundly obligated to the doctrine Granville-Barker enunciated in his essay on *Love's Labor's Lost*:

The actor, in fine, must think of the dialogue in terms of music; of the tune and rhythm of it as at one with the sense—sometimes outbidding the sense—in telling him what to do and how to do it, in telling him, indeed, what to *be*.

A City Center production in New York in 1953 gave the play a quasi-Oscar Wilde tone but with very turn-of-the-century furnishings—the ladies made their entrance in an ancient roadster, there was a gramophone with a great horn, a crooked croquet game, pleasing some critics but not Wolcott Gibbs and Brooks Atkinson. Brook's principles had gone astray, as they were to in several of the new ventures. What might have sustained the satirical intent of the play sometimes ended in travesty, as one may judge in Bernard Beckerman's account of the 1968 production in Stratford, Connecticut:

> The academy was the retreat of a guru. Berowne, Longaville, and Dumaine were fashionable young men come to share the retreat with the Maharishi King of Navarre. Probably stimulated by the adventures of the Beatles in yoga-land, Dumaine turned out to be a rock-singer. Holofernes, in what I assume to be a parody of Mahatma Gandhi, wore silver-rimmed spectacles and a diaper-like sheet. And the ladies of France were cycle-riding, fast-moving members of the jet-set, chaperoned by a swishing Boyet chattering in a deep South drawl.

The BBC telecast in 1985 developed a similar kind of transformation, but on this occasion the television frame itself set limits on what can be done pictorially with what was originally a stage play. As the producer saw it, this limitation precluded any disposition to offer settings in the open country or in a park. The beautiful pastoral setting was obliterated, the Academy and the pavilion became, the reviewer said, "a cold-lit library, across whose chilly spaces—littered with frigid statuary and leathern tomes—tread bewigged would-be *philosophes*."

Recently the wheel seems to have come full circle in the

1984 production of the Royal Shakespeare Company, or so it seemed to Giles Gordon:

> To me, *Love's Labor's Lost* is one of the supreme glories of dramatic art, the equal of that most essential of operas, Mozart's *Così fan Tutte.* The wit, brio and erudition of the verbal music are marvelous to experience. The stage is washed in white leaves which, from the first entrance of the princess of France and her court, suggests spring until the end, the arrival of the Messenger of Death, when Autumn gives way to Winter and icicles hang by the wall, and Dick the shepherd blows his nail.

Pace Brook, the sequential is once again at the heart of the play, although it is only fair to observe that the costumes were nineteenth century and the setting Chekhovian.

Quite as significant as the experimenting that followed Brook's example was the increasing recognition of the excellence of the play, as theater and as poetry. It was put into the hands of the best actors and actresses—Olivier, Derek Jacobi, Joan Plowright, Ian Richardson, Paul Scofield, to single out but a few. Again and again the word "exquisite" is applied to the conceits and humor that engage the characters, to the sequences that call for dance-like movements—not only in the mask but from the very beginning, as in the San Diego production of 1962, described by Eleanor Prosser:

> The brilliant choreography of Shirlee Dodge combined with creative direction to make this the artistic triumph of the season. The high style of dance was established in the opening scenes. To the accompaniment of music from the balcony, servants scurried from the center curtains in balanced patterns, setting up an abacus, a telescope, and a globe. The dance movement and the pretty artificiality of the props (a powder-blue telescope?) against a background of crystalline trees set the stage for Navarre's foolish game.

And at the end the musical impetus was irresistible:

Accompanied solely by Don Armado on the tabor and
two lonely recorders, the cast sang of the owl and the
cuckoo while the lovers moved through a series of
measured dances. Bernard Windt had written new music
for the song, two haunting melodies in a minor key, sung
first in unison, then antiphonally by the divided cast
banked on each side of the stage, and then together in a
round. As the singers and the song faded through the
side doors and the light gradually dimmed, one by one
each couple parted in the center, still in dance, until
finally only Rosaline and Berowne were left—each paus-
ing at the side door for a final look and a gentle salute
of promise and yet regret, before leaving the stage to
hushed darkness and the night.

And finally, as so much talent and intelligence were
lavished upon a play that had been so long neglected, so
the humor and the wordplay that had once been supposed
to be a drawback came to be understood as wonderfully
effective dramatically. No one has pointed this out better
than Richard David, unless it be the actors themselves,
such as Paul Scofield and Tony Church:

> David Jones, it seemed to me in the 1973 production of
> the Royal Shakespeare Company, had seized the essential
> fact that Shakespeare's comic effects are almost always
> very strongly visual; get these visual effects right, and
> the words will fall into place of themselves. Take one
> of the simplest, Armado and Moth: the basic jest is the
> mere juxtaposition of the lofty, slow-moving, and solemn
> Spaniard with his diminutive quicksilver page. The verb-
> al altercations between Armado and Moth are little more
> than elaborations of the fundamental contrast between
> dignity and impudence. Or take the scene where Jacque-
> netta asks the Parson to interpret Berowne's letter which
> was mistakenly delivered to her instead of to Rosaline.
> The schoolmaster, convinced that he is the only man
> present who is competent to deal with the written word,
> itches to be involved but has to pretend to be thinking of
> higher things while he edges himself into the act. His
> impatience, his various mumming routines to cover his

real intentions, and his efforts to look over the Parson's shoulder, are *visual* comedy. . . . The essentials of these and other comic scenes were given so clear a visual projection that they were able to carry any amount of verbal superstructure.

In short, the recent history of the play upon the stage justifies the judgment made upon it as beautifully and wonderfully conceived. But it has been a rocky road, and in some aspects still is. In 1733 when Theobald completed his edition of the play he wrote in exasperation: "I have now done with this Play, which in the Main may be call'd a very bad One: and I have found it so very troublesome in the Corruptions, that, I think, I may conclude with the old religious Editors, *Deo gratias!*" As for some of the modern versions, the reception has been less than complimentary, as W. L. Godshalk summarizes: "The more recent productions of *Love's Labor's Lost*, especially those of the 1960's and 1970's, are marked by a general distrust of the play on its merits, for what it attempts to say and its ability to do so." Godshalk gives examples, and then says:

> Such corruptions of the text seem to imply that the productions become, in the words of Vincent Canby, " 'such a flat denial of the original that it becomes an elaborate apology for anyone's being caught alive doing the play'."
> Brooks Atkinson was no more forgiving: "After a glimpse of *Love's Labor's Lost*, which opened at the City Center last evening, it is easy to see why this Shakespearean comedy had not been played since 1891."

All the same it is certain that the play now has a secure place in the repertory. Colleges and universities as well as the professional theaters are putting it on, many of the productions truly imaginative. It is increasingly understood that this comic treatment of some cultivated young bloods, as Granville-Barker spoke of them, is as rich in intellectuality as in antics, and that the gloriously beautiful song at the end has been prepared for by a sustained articulation of ideas.

Suggested References

The number of possible references is vast and grows alarmingly. (The *Shakespeare Quarterly* devotes one issue each year to a list of the previous year's work, and *Shakespeare Survey*—an annual publication—includes a substantial review of recent scholarship, as well as an occasional essay surveying a few decades of scholarship on a chosen topic.) Though no works are indispensable, those listed below have been found especially helpful.

1. Shakespeare's Times

Byrne, M. St. Clare. *Elizabethan Life in Town and Country.* Rev. ed. New York: Barnes & Noble, 1961. Chapters on manners, beliefs, education, etc., with illustrations.

Joseph, B. L. *Shakespeare's Eden: The Commonwealth of England, 1558–1629.* New York: Barnes & Noble, 1971. An account of the social, political, economic, and cultural life of England.

Schoenbaum, S. *Shakespeare: The Globe and the World.* New York: Oxford University Press, 1979. A readable, handsomely illustrated book on the world of the Elizabethans.

Shakespeare's England. 2 vols. Oxford: Oxford University Press, 1916. A large collection of scholarly essays on a wide variety of topics (e.g. astrology, costume, gardening, horsemanship), with special attention to Shakespeare's references to these topics.

Stone, Lawrence. *The Crisis of the Aristocracy, 1558–1641,* abridged edition. London: Oxford University Press, 1967.

2. Shakespeare

Barnet, Sylvan. *A Short Guide to Shakespeare.* New York: Harcourt Brace Jovanovich, 1974. An introduction to all of the works and to the dramatic traditions behind them.

Bentley, Gerald E. *Shakespeare: A Biographical Handbook.* New Haven, Conn.: Yale University Press, 1961. The facts about Shakespeare, with virtually no conjecture intermingled.

Bush, Geoffrey. *Shakespeare and the Natural Condition.* Cambridge, Mass.: Harvard University Press, 1956. A short, sensitive account of Shakespeare's view of "Nature," touching most of the works.

Chambers, E. K. *William Shakespeare: A Study of Facts and Problems.* 2 vols. London: Oxford University Press, 1930. An invaluable, detailed reference work; not for the casual reader.

Chute, Marchette. *Shakespeare of London.* New York: Dutton, 1949. A readable biography fused with portraits of Stratford and London life.

Clemen, Wolfgang H. *The Development of Shakespeare's Imagery.* Cambridge, Mass.: Harvard University Press, 1951. (Originally published in German, 1936.) A temperate account of a subject often abused.

Granville-Barker, Harley. *Prefaces to Shakespeare.* 2 vols. Princeton, N. J.: Princeton University Press, 1946–47. Essays on ten plays by a scholarly man of the theater.

Harbage, Alfred. *As They Liked It.* New York: Macmillan, 1947. A long, sensitive essay on Shakespeare, morality, and the audience's expectations.

Kernan, Alvin B., ed. *Modern Shakespearean Criticism: Essays on Style, Dramaturgy, and the Major Plays.* New York: Harcourt Brace Jovanovich, 1970. A collection of major formalist criticism.

————. "The Plays and the Playwrights." In *The Revels History of Drama in English,* general editors Clifford Leech and T. W. Craik. Vol. III. London: Methuen, 1975. A book-length essay surveying Elizabethan drama with substantial discussions of Shakespeare's plays.

Schoenbaum, S. *Shakespeare's Lives.* Oxford: Clarendon Press, 1970. A review of the evidence, and an examination of many biographies, including those by Baconians and other heretics.

————. *William Shakespeare: A Compact Documentary Life.* New York: Oxford University Press, 1977. A readable presentation of all that the documents tell us about Shakespeare.

Traversi, D. A. *An Approach to Shakespeare.* 3rd rev. ed., 2 vols. New York: Doubleday, 1968–69. An analysis of the plays beginning with words, images, and themes, rather than with characters.

Van Doren, Mark. *Shakespeare.* New York: Holt, 1939. Brief, perceptive readings of all of the plays.

3. Shakespeare's Theater

Beckerman, Bernard. *Shakespeare at the Globe, 1599–1609.* New York: Macmillan, 1962. On the playhouse and on Elizabethan dramaturgy, acting, and staging.

Chambers, E. K. *The Elizabethan Stage.* 4 vols. New York: Oxford University Press, 1945. A major reference work on theaters, theatrical companies, and staging at court.

Cook, Ann Jennalie. *The Privileged Playgoers of Shakespeare's London, 1576–1642.* Princeton, N. J.: Princeton University Press, 1981. Sees Shakespeare's audience as more middle-class and more intellectual than Harbage (below) does.

Gurr, Andrew. *The Shakespearean Stage: 1574–1642.* 2d edition. Cambridge: Cambridge University Press, 1981. On the acting companies, the actors, the playhouses, the stages, and the audiences.

Harbage, Alfred. *Shakespeare's Audience.* New York: Columbia University Press, 1941. A study of the size and nature of the theatrical public, emphasizing its representativeness.

Hodges, C. Walter. *The Globe Restored.* London: Ernest Benn, 1953. A well-illustrated and readable attempt to reconstruct the Globe Theatre.

Hosley, Richard. "The Playhouses." In *The Revels History of Drama in English,* general editors Clifford Leech and T. W. Craik. Vol. III. London: Methuen, 1975. An essay of one hundred pages on the physical aspects of the playhouses.

Kernodle, George R. *From Art to Theatre: Form and Convention in the Renaissance.* Chicago: University of Chicago Press, 1944. Pioneering and stimulating work on the symbolic and cultural meaning of theater construction.

Nagler, A. M. *Shakespeare's Stage.* Trans. Ralph Manheim. New Haven, Conn.: Yale University Press, 1958. A very brief introduction to the physical aspects of the playhouse.

Slater, Ann Pasternak. *Shakespeare the Director.* Totowa, N. J.: Barnes & Noble, 1982. An analysis of theatrical effects (e.g., kissing, kneeling) in stage directions and dialogue.

Thomson, Peter. *Shakespeare Theatre.* London: Routledge & Kegan Paul, 1983. A discussion of how plays were staged in Shakespeare's time.

4. Miscellaneous Reference Works

Abbott, E. A. *A Shakespearean Grammar.* New Edition. New York: Macmillan, 1877. An examination of differences between Elizabethan and modern grammar.

Bevington, David. *Shakespeare.* Arlington Heights, Ill.: A. H. M. Publishing, 1978. A short guide to hundreds of important writings on the works.

Bullough, Geoffrey. *Narrative and Dramatic Sources of Shakespeare.* 8 vols. New York: Columbia University Press, 1957–75. A collection of many of the books Shakespeare drew upon, with judicious comments.

Campbell, Oscar James, and Edward G. Quinn. *The Reader's Encyclopedia of Shakespeare.* New York: Crowell, 1966. More than 2,600 entries, from a few sentences to a few pages, on everything related to Shakespeare.

Greg, W. W. *The Shakespeare First Folio.* New York: Oxford University Press, 1955. A detailed yet readable history of the first collection (1623) of Shakespeare's plays.

Kökeritz, Helge. *Shakespeare's Names.* New Haven, Conn.: Yale University Press, 1959. A guide to the pronunciation of some 1,800 names appearing in Shakespeare.

———. *Shakespeare's Pronunciation.* New Haven, Conn.: Yale University Press, 1953. Contains much information about puns and rhymes.

Muir, Kenneth. *The Sources of Shakespeare's Plays.* New Haven, Conn.: Yale University Press, 1978. An account of Shakespeare's use of his reading.

The Norton Facsimile: The First Folio of Shakespeare. Prepared by Charles Hinman. New York: Norton, 1968. A handsome and accurate facsimile of the first collection (1623) of Shakespeare's plays.

Onions, C. T. *A Shakespeare Glossary*. 2d ed., rev., with
enlarged addenda. London: Oxford University Press, 1953.
Definitions of words (or senses of words) now obsolete.

Partridge, Eric. *Shakespeare's Bawdy*. Rev. ed. New York:
Dutton, 1955. A glossary of bawdy words and phrases.

Shakespeare Quarterly. See headnote to Suggested References.

Shakespeare Survey. See headnote to Suggested References.

Shakespeare's Plays in Quarto. A Facsimile Edition. Ed.
Michael J. B. Allen and Kenneth Muir. Berkeley, Calif.:
University of California Press, 1981. A book of nine
hundred pages, containing facsimiles of twenty-two of the
quarto editions of Shakespeare's plays. An invaluable
complement to *The Norton Facsimile: The First Folio of
Shakespeare* (see above).

Smith, Gordon Ross. *A Classified Shakespeare Bibliography
1936–1958*. University Park, Pa.: Pennsylvania State University Press, 1963. A list of some twenty thousand items
on Shakespeare.

Spevack, Marvin. *The Harvard Concordance to Shakespeare*.
Cambridge, Mass.: Harvard University Press, 1973. An
index to Shakespeare's words.

Wells, Stanley, ed. *Shakespeare: Select Bibliographies*. London: Oxford University Press. 1973. Seventeen essays
surveying scholarship and criticism of Shakespeare's life,
work, and theater.

5. *Love's Labor's Lost*

Arthos, John. *Shakespeare: The Early Writings*. London:
Bowes & Bowes, 1972.

Baldwin, T. W. *Shakspere's Five-Act Structure: Shakspere's
Early Plays on the Background of Renaissance Theories of
Five-Act Structure from 1470*. Urbana, Illinois: University
of Illinois Press, 1947.

Barber, C. L. *Shakespeare's Festive Comedy*. Princeton, N.J.:
Princeton University Press, 1959.

Bradbrook, M. C. *The School of Night. Study in the Literary
Relationships of Sir Walter Raleigh*. Cambridge: Cambridge University Press, 1936.

Carroll, W. C. *The Great Feast of Language in Love's*

Labour's Lost. Princeton, N.J.: Princeton University Press, 1976.

Harvey, N. L., and Carey, A. K. *Love's Labor's Lost, An Annotated Bibliography*. New York and London: Garland Publishers, 1984.

Homans, Sidney. *When the Theater Turns to Itself*. Lewisburg, Pa.: Bucknell University Press, 1981.

Hoy, Cyrus. *The Hyacinth Room*. New York: Knopf, 1964.

Kerrigan, John. "Shakespeare at Work: The Katharine Rosaline Tangle in *Love's Labour's Lost*," *Review of English Studies*, 33 (1982), 129–36.

Lamb, Mary Ellen. "The Nature of Topicality in *Love's Labour's Lost*," *Shakespeare Survey 38* (1985), 49–59.

Montrose, L. A. *"Curious-Knotted Garden": The Form, Themes, and Contexts of Shakespeare's "Love's Labour's Lost."* Salzburg: Universität Salzburg, 1977.

Palmer, J. L. *Comic Characters of Shakespeare*. London: Macmillan, 1946.

Parson, Philip. "Shakespeare and the Mask," *Shakespeare Survey 16*, 121–31.

Roesen, Bobbyann, "Love's Labour's Lost," *Shakespeare Quarterly*, 4 (1953), 411–26.

Taylor, Rupert. *The Date of "Love's Labor's Lost."* New York: AMS Press, 1966.

Vyvyan, John. *Shakespeare and the Rose of Love*. New York: Barnes & Noble, 1960; London: Chatto & Windus, 1960.

Wells, Stanley. "The Copy for the Folio Text of *Love's Labour's Lost*," *Review of English Studies*, 33 (1982), 137–47.

Westlund, Joseph. "Fancy and Achievement in *Love's Labour's Lost*," *Shakespeare Quarterly*, 18 (1967), 37–46.

Wilson, J. D. *Shakespeare's Happy Comedies*. London: Faber and Faber, 1962.

Yates, F. A. *A Study of "Love's Labour's Lost."* Cambridge: Cambridge University Press, 1936.